THE
TRAGEDY
IN THE
WORKPLACE

*"Seen not in your
local theaters,
but in every
business in America"*

THE
TRAGEDY
IN THE
WORKPLACE

The Longest Running
Show in the Country

by

Danna Beal, M.Ed.

A publication of Destiny Publishing and Danna Beal Consulting, LLC.

Published by Luminary Media Group, an imprint of Pine Orchard, Inc.
Visit us on the internet at www.pineorchard.com

Printed in Canada.

ISBN 1-930580-05-3

In memory of
RODNEY EDWARD GANNON,
an enlightened leader.

Dedicated to my parents,
DANIEL "BUD" GATES
and
MARGARET "PEGGY" MEENACH GATES.

Also, to my son and daughter,
KYLE and STEPHANIE,
for their ever-abiding love,
faith, and trust in me.

CONTENTS

PART I: THE CURRENT WORKPLACE

CHAPTER ONE
THE TRAGEDY OCCURRING IN TODAY'S BUSINESSES

CHAPTER TWO
WHAT IS ENLIGHTENED LEADERSHIP?

CHAPTER THREE
THE STAGE AND THE PASSIONATE DRAMA IN THE WORKPLACE

PART II: SHINING THE SPOTLIGHT ON THE STAGE AT WORK

CHAPTER FOUR
THE STAR (PROTAGONIST) AND THEME

CHAPTER FIVE
MOTIVE AND PLOT

CHAPTER SIX
THE DIRECTOR AND SCRIPT

CHAPTER SEVEN
THE CAMERA: THE LENS AND FILTER OF JUDGMENT

CHAPTER EIGHT
THE ENEMY (ANTAGONIST) AND THE CONFLICT

PART III: AWAKENING FROM THE DRAMA

CHAPTER NINE
ENLIGHTENED LEADERSHIP

CHAPTER TEN
THE FINAL PERFORMANCE

PURPOSE

This book is about rebuilding relationships in the workplace by honoring the spirit in ourselves and in others, residing beneath our self-created identities that are battling and competing for power and validation. This shallow interpretation of ourselves, a shabby imitation we have come to believe is true, belies our incredible authentic power. One day, when fear can be replaced with trust and compassion for one another, there will be a shift in consciousness. People everywhere will be restored to their true identities, their inner spiritual greatness that was intended by the Creator. To that end, this book is dedicated.

ACKNOWLEDGMENTS

I humbly acknowledge those people whose roles in my life have profoundly touched me and taught me who I am:

John Pilley for being the mirror to my deepest fears and pains, for helping me with my destiny of bringing spirit and compassion to the workplace and, finally, for teaching me to honor myself.

Pat Carey, my soul sister. Our early morning conversations on the Stairmaster, as we shared our spiritual evolution, our laughter, and our tears, were invaluable to this work.

Bob Beale (no relative, but a dear friend) for his mentoring and his spiritual support in life as well as business.

My wonderful sister, Nancy Martin, and my two supportive friends, Sharon Leonard and Karen Corkery, who came forth like angels when I needed them.

Frank and Cindy Sadler, whose friendship and deep conversations contributed to my book, my seminars, and my life.

Peter Martinelli and Chris Deviny, who trusted me with their open hearts and souls.

Pat Keas, Robin and Scott Houston, Vivyan Strong, my family, friends, associates, and all the other players on my life stage with whom I have interacted.

You have all contributed to my life's work.

Never doubt that a small group of thoughtfully committed citizens can change the world; indeed, it is the only thing that ever has.

—Margaret Mead

INTRODUCTION

I have been a business consultant, speaker, and seminar leader for nearly twenty years in the Pacific Northwest. During this time, I have worked with a wide variety of businesses and organizations, and have spoken at and attended conferences around the Unites States. I have worked with almost every industry including hospitals, physician practices, CPA firms, law firms, auto dealerships, banks, restaurants, museums, construction firms, retirement centers, retail stores, non-profit agencies, schools, fitness clubs, insurance agencies, and numerous small businesses.

Sadly, I have come to one overriding conclusion: there is an enormous tragedy occurring in the workplace today.

The present working environment is fraught with fears and envy, egos competing for validation and attention, managers who disempower employees, co-workers who hurt and sabotage one another, and, most insidious of all, an underlying fear that permeates the atmosphere with insecurity and indecision.

Do you think this is an exaggeration?

I assure you, it is not. I have seen and felt unbearable pain in the faces and words of the people who describe to me their workplace. The work environment today has never been more combative and filled with emotional turbulence. It is almost amazing that any work is accomplished, considering all the distractions. I am going to suggest that most business productivity and achievement is actually motivated by fear rather than inspiration. Consider the possibilities for new levels of business success and advancement if we had an environment of compassion, respect, and freedom.

While working with many different organizations, I have seen prejudices, harassment, political and territorial battles, selfishness, grandiosity, betrayal, and suffering—all a result of disempowered human beings trying to elevate themselves at the expense of others. Gossip by both men and women is rampant, and power struggles between individuals and groups are occurring at all levels—from the CEOs down. Gossip provides temporary relief from pain by sharing misery and giving a sense of power to those engaged in it. Gossip, even as it appears to temporarily relieve some pain in the individuals, does so at the cost of adding more negativity and uncertainty to the working environment.

Some people are actually energized by the competitive environment. This, however, is only temporary because fear and mistrust always accompany the competitive environment. Deception and suspicion are prevalent, and the ever-present shadow of anxiety is lurking in the background. Emotions are suppressed. People are psychologically out of balance.

So the workplace has become a combat or war zone with people suffering from incredible stress and "dis-ease" in the very place they believe is providing them security. And finally, so great is the fear of losing job security, many people cannot readily admit, even to themselves, that the situation is that traumatic.

Why is all this turbulence in the workplace occurring?

It is the ego's efforts to overcome its own sense of powerlessness in the face of so many rapid changes in the local and global business environment. The expansion of new technology, the creation of an instantaneous mode of communication, and the high-paced style of businesses today have all added to the sense of exhaustion and helplessness. People feel that they, literally, cannot "keep up."

People everywhere have a sense of being lost in the storm, feeling insignificant and hopeless. The inner sense of authentic power and confidence needed to withstand this pressure are obscured by fear, fatigue, and the ever-present cutthroat attitude of bosses and co-workers. Many people are leaving the employment environment in favor of self-employment or the newly emerging "home-based" business. Those options require the courage and ability to take risks, and that is difficult to generate when one is supporting a family.

This harried and impersonal environment has resulted in a variety of behaviors by people attempting to cope and to reduce fear. These efforts are actually methods to disguise and prevent pain. The projection, blame, gossip, back stabbing, manipulation, and other dysfunctional behaviors are all attempts by the ego to deny the deep lack of self-worth. These attempts to bolster the ego are futile strategies to mask insecurity and alleviate anxiety.

The response from both managers and employees of various organizations is a resounding "yes" that this situation has, indeed, reached critical proportions. The crisis doesn't exist just in some organizations and businesses, but it is actually occurring in nearly every single business throughout the country. Today, people are crying out for a solution and anxiously praying for some relief from this massive dilemma.

People are spiritually hungry and emotionally depleted. They do not know how to escape from the misery experienced in the very place that they spend three-fourths of their waking hours. It is a double-edged sword: they feel they must depend on the organization to provide their economic security and yet, staying in the organization is also causing them enormous levels of anxiety and pain. Many people feel immobilized. Counselors and physicians are seeing a growing number of desperate and unhealthy people due to job stress.

I believe I have developed a model that will make a significant difference in the workplace by bringing clarity to the present situation of entangled personalities. My model provides a method for understanding and breaking through the intense drama. Those engaged in the drama are unable to discern the underlying causes of the confusion and resentment. The solution is actually simple but very obtuse. They are too deeply involved to see the whole picture.

In this book, I will share with you a framework that illuminates and simplifies the complexity of this web of reacting and counter-reacting egos that has reached a crisis level in businesses today. The model will help you discover a way of operating from authentic power rather than from the fragile power of the ego. It is then a process of "doing" and demonstrating this new way of interacting with the people with whom you work. The results will be the proof. The positive outcome will be recognized and perpetuated. It will cause a domino effect in the workplace, and it will be self-rewarding to those who commit to and practice this unique approach.

The workplace can actually provide many opportunities for learning and evolution because life lessons are presented in relationships. Because of the repeated interactions in the workplace, egos are often hooked, resulting in suffering, anger, projection, and self-doubt. The frequency of the interactions with the same people over and over again results in emotions and reactions becoming intensified.

The good news is that these confrontations and painful experiences can provide possibilities for one to learn about oneself and to begin the process of healing the soul. I believe that is our life purpose—to rediscover the peace and joy that is inherently ours. Interactions that bring up pain and anxiety within us can also lead us to discover the source of the problem, so we can release it and become free.

However, it is not easy to give up the demands of the ego because our ego will do anything to protect its false identity. We find it personally humiliating to let go of our ego's needs because we fear doing so will diminish the image we have of ourselves. Since our ego is dependent upon the reactions of others to validate itself and to reinforce its identity, we do not give up this emotional turmoil easily, even when it is causing immense suffering.

My book is intended to help create a transformation in the leadership of businesses first, which will then make it safer for the employees to also begin the process. Although anyone, anytime, can begin to stop playing the automatic part in the scenes being played out by other egos in the workplace, it is generally easier for those in leadership positions to start the process. They have more "perceived" power and security.

Through my model, it will become clear that facing and then challenging the ego are the only ways to peace. My book is intended to help people step off the stage of the long-running tragedy in the workplace. Discovering your inner strength by letting go of fear will lead you to genuine happiness and satisfaction. The goals of my book are two-fold: short term— heal the pain; long term—heal the soul.

GETTING TO THE SOURCE OF THE POWER STRUGGLES

How does this change come about in the tightly woven drama of intertwined egos? Something has to occur to begin the process. My goal is to introduce a unique way to shed light on the core causes and the fundamental reasons for the power struggles and territorial battles. The leaders, the business managers, or owners can then begin the process of unraveling the closely-knit mesh of egos in the workplace. Those being led are usually too disempowered and wounded to initiate the process.

This book is not a simple "how to" course on the steps to becoming a good leader. I have found that most courses and books on leadership are instructions on how to change behavior and how to "act" like a leader. This book is a course on teaching you to discover and release the barriers that prevent the inner qualities of authentic and enlightened leadership from emerging.

It is my observation that most leaders in all sizes of organizations are operating from the ego, rather than from authentic power. The ego blocks the true creativity and energy that could be released in the workplace.

The symptoms of an ego-driven management style include the following:

- Personal agendas rather than the common good of the organization are the order of the day.
- Conditioning from past fears and disappointments is the basis for decisions.
- External validation such as money, status, and power are the motivators.
- Projection and blame, rather than ownership and personal responsibility, are the norm.
- Fear is the underlying factor for all action by an ego-driven leader.

A change in the ego-driven management style is necessary. What does it take for leaders to make this transformation?

It requires the willingness of leaders to look with an unflinching eye at the inadequacies of their own egos. That, indeed, takes great courage.

This book will aid in finding freedom from the ego, the self-created identity that is the source of all the endless battles occurring in almost every business everywhere. Becoming an enlightened business leader demands disengaging from the insane drama and creating an environment of peace, harmony, and compassion.

Because of the current ego-driven management, many people in the workplace feel as though they are in prison, with little freedom of expression or ability to perform and contribute at their highest level. Learning to face the ego and learning to become an enlightened leader are meaningful and necessary goals. As business leaders begin to personally transform, they will free the employees to work creatively and productively within an environment that fosters their true potential.

As leaders give up the ego needs of superiority, employees will lay down the ego defenses and complaints of the downtrodden. People will learn to give up blaming others for their circumstances and take back their own destinies. As leaders elevate their own understanding, they will be models for those they lead. Those they lead will find liberation and discover their own inner power.

I believe the ability to transcend the drama can only come about when one connects with the inner spirit and acknowledges that same spirit in others. Giving up the ego and its demands, however, is very difficult and will take commitment and determination. The ego's goal is to keep fear below the surface and to convince you and others that it is invincible (which, of course, it is not). Getting someone to give up the demands of the ego is like trying to take a favorite toy away from a child who is grasping it tightly. The ego is not given up without a battle.

The conflict becomes ego versus spirit.

That is a most formidable battle because the ego is relentless and deceptive in its desire to remain in charge. But as you persevere, the grip of the ego will diminish and the spiritual strength will begin to replace the artificial power of the ego.

Like anything new, it will take practice and you will have some trials and errors in the workplace. But gradually, the results will become apparent. People will begin to communicate on a deeply honest and respectful level when they feel trust and integrity in the environment. Gossip and sabotage will become a thing of the past as people begin this process of changing internally and accepting personal responsibility. They will enjoy coming to work, sharing mutual goals, and feeling the satisfaction of a job well done.

Businesses will reach new levels of success as the synergy of teamwork is allowed to emerge in an environment where trust and compassion prevail. Employees will start to feel loyalty once again, and the organizations will attract and retain the kind of people they desire. Cooperation without suspicion will return to the workplace. When people are no longer expending energy in battles with one another, new vigor and vitality will become available for positive production and success. This positive force of human dynamics has been so restricted in the current environment.

I invite you to join me in the worthwhile endeavor of rebuilding relationships in the workplace so that people everywhere will have a better quality of life. The workplace is a place where millions of people come face to face with the issues within themselves that need healing. Let us use the opportunity to rediscover who we are and be restored to our inner greatness. As the workplace atmosphere becomes peaceful, our families, communities, social structures, governments, and future generations will be affected. We will begin to experience the inner joy, peace, and contentment that we desire and deserve.

A human being is a part of the whole,
called by us the "Universe," a part limited in
time and space. He experiences himself, his
thoughts and feelings as something separate
from the rest—a kind of optical illusion of his
consciousness. This delusion is a kind of prison
for us, restricting us to our personal desires and
to affection for a few persons nearest to us. Our
task must be to free ourselves from the prison by
widening our circle of compassion to embrace
all living creatures and the whole of nature in
its beauty. Nobody is able to achieve this
completely, but the striving for such achievement
is in itself a part of the liberation and a
foundation for inner security.

—Albert Einstein

PART I

THE CURRENT
WORKPLACE

CHAPTER ONE

The Tragedy Occurring in Today's Businesses

PEOPLE ARE SUFFERING

This book is about a restoration process: the restoration of you to your authentic self, and the restoration of the workplace to an environment of trust and compassion.

People are suffering everywhere in businesses and organizations because they are operating from wounded egos, in environments of fear, rather than trust and compassion.

In my seminars and workshops on enlightened leadership, I begin by asking people from the audience to share their description and perspective of the workplace environment. These participants are leaders and managers from a wide variety of businesses, organizations, and government.

Here are their descriptions, descriptions of the workplace environment from all different industries and levels of management:

- ◆ Paranoia
- ◆ Egos
- ◆ Gossip
- ◆ Insecurity
- ◆ Lack of appreciation
- ◆ Power struggles
- ◆ Secretive
- ◆ Hidden and personal agendas
- ◆ Intimidation

- Unpredictable
- Workaholism
- Fear
- Blame
- Turf protection
- Lack of trust
- Lack of communication
- Sabotaging
- All kinds of discrimination (sexual preference, gender, race, religion, economic groups, size, etc.)

Does that sound like a wonderful place to spend eight to ten hours a day, five to six days a week? Yet that is what people are doing!

Keep in mind: the above comments are from leadership seminars. However, employees and lower-level staff have the same complaints—only amplified, and they have less power to bring about change.

As a consultant to businesses, I begin new engagements by conducting an information-gathering session with each member of the organization's management and staff that I am assisting. These sessions are confidential so that I can assess the organization, its culture, its needs, and its goals from a variety of viewpoints.

Individuals who are in pain often reveal to me, the outside consultant, that which they would not share with the leadership in the organization. Repeatedly, I have heard men and women, managers and staff, individually describe to me the stress and suffering of working in their current environment.

It is not the job or the work that they dislike. In fact, most people actually enjoy the work itself; and people, inherently, do want to do a good job. It is the "politics," the undercurrent of biases and power struggles, the fear, insecurity, and lack of trust in the environment that is causing the pain.

In general, employees express feeling unappreciated, left out of decisions, suspicious of fellow employees, and exhausted from being unable to meet the workload demand.

In addition, they convey little loyalty as they often feel the management does not care about them. They describe management as interested in them only as a tool to make more money for the owners or for the highest-level management. They often feel their job could be eliminated and that management has no loyalty toward them.

The managers are distrustful of other managers and wary of those they manage. Fear of others outperforming and replacing them is a very common fear, although not easily admitted. The individuals at all levels state a desire for improvement in the environment, a need for teamwork, and a hope for relief from stress.

However, most people indicate a sense of resignation, a sense of despair. They communicate an attitude of "that's just the way it is and it probably won't change." Many individuals admit to me that they are actually keeping their eye out for another job opportunity somewhere else where they believe they would find a better environment.

Unfortunately, they will usually discover the same scenario wherever they go.

THE EMPLOYEE'S PERCEPTION
OF THE WORKPLACE

Let's look more closely at the workplace from the perspective of employees. The world of an employee, working in a company where spirit and compassion are not present in the leadership, looks like this:

On Sunday, I am often depressed thinking of returning to the harshness of yet another day at a workplace that I find uncertain and unsatisfying at best, miserable and intolerable at worst. I try to deny this because I am dependent upon the job to financially survive. I convince myself and others that my job is tolerable.

At work, I am unaware of the company's mission. And if there is a mission, I had no input into it, so why should I have any personal commitment to it? [Research has shown that employee input into the company's mission is an important component to job satisfaction.] *I don't feel "in the know." Communication from management is incomplete and inconsistent, and there is often a sense of secrecy. There is an unspoken agreement that many issues and topics are unapproachable or not open to discussion.*

There are some camaraderie and efforts to appreciate others, demonstrated by celebrations, employee recognition events, picnics, birthdays, etc. but it is often tinged with a sense of tension and lack of authenticity. And lying under the surface is the actual lack of trust felt toward management, as well as each other, which creates a constant uneasiness and unrest. Most everyone feels an undercurrent of rivalry, although it is rarely admitted or addressed.

I may be a good producer or a very high performer, but it is often the result of the fear of being replaced or being overlooked rather than positive motivation. That brings about the most common complaint that is heard in most every work environment, including my own: "I feel unappreciated. I'm rarely thanked or acknowledged for a job well done."

I'm expected to provide outstanding service for the company, and yet I feel, out of integrity, that I'm obligated in trying to project something outward that is not practiced from within my company. I feel like a hypocrite, trying to represent a standard that is not operating internally. I wonder why management doesn't "practice what they preach."

Because I feel I really have no voice, after my initial phase of employment, I have given up trying to express concerns or make a difference in my workplace. Besides, issues about this are rarely acknowledged. Even if they are, little is done to address them and nothing really changes. I have become resigned to how things are and have stopped trying to contribute when my work is not recognized or received with good intention.

My viewpoint of management is that the company is out to just make money, create personal power, and look after its own interests. As a result, I have very little allegiance to its leadership. When another opportunity for me opens up elsewhere, I will be gone in a flash, leaving everyone surprised because of the unexpressed misery.

Of course, not wanting to burn bridges, I may not express my true feelings about the workplace or the reason for leaving. Management will be relieved to hear that it was not the company's fault and quickly will move on to hire my replacement, never examining what lesson might have been learned or what could have been done differently to have kept me. On the other hand, perhaps the management will hold it against me for leaving—a simple case of projection of the problem onto anyone but itself.

Meanwhile, in this depressing workplace environment, I leave at the end of the day, exhausted and unsatisfied with the work completed, but happy that the day has ended. Hump day (Wednesday) I embrace with enthusiasm, as I look forward to Friday and relief from the exhausting, endless grind of my job. The weekend flies by and Sunday is upon me once again, almost ruined at some point in the day or evening when I begin to think of returning to work on Monday.

This perception of being a victim is coming from the wounded ego that cannot see its participation in this sufferable situation. Employees feel that they have no voice and, therefore, believe nothing can be done to alter the situation. Employees, because of their perceived lack of power, are usually not able to make significant differences, so they resort to other methods for coping in the unhappy workplace.

Since the employee feels little power, any real change in the workplace will most often need to come from the leadership. That is not to say that an employee cannot be the one to begin the process of unhooking from the company's ongoing power struggles. But that's only if the employee begins to see the truth—the powerlessness of the egos running the company. In fact, the employee is often able to see the "Emperor Wore No Clothes" scenario, but is usually too frightened to try to impact the dynamics of the management for fear of repercussions.

It is much more far-reaching and influential when the lessons of giving up the needs of the ego are done first by the leadership of the organization. This is because leaders have more power to change the environment than those being led.

UNDERSTANDING THE EGO

An understanding of the ego, in the sense I am using it, is important here. Enlightened leadership requires beginning the process of becoming free of some constraints of the ego. The ego is a self-created identity, which is a small portion of who we are destined to become. It is a role that we project into the world to create an image we think is desirable. It helps us cope in uncertain situations, gets us what we think we need, and keeps us safe.

It is not real, but merely a way of defining who we are that we believe will get us through life, with as little bruising and suffering as possible. The ego unconsciously senses that it is really very small and does not want this discovered by yourself or others. It is very insecure and looks outside itself to find security and support for its role in the world.

The powerlessness of the ego is difficult to recognize because it is such a good actor.

Unfortunately, the path of the ego is actually the way to inevitable suffering and it always leads to the same conclusion. But the denial by the ego is so strong and impenetrable that we usually won't believe that the ego is leading us astray until the pain reaches intolerable levels. The ego has been running our lives so long it is difficult to even discover that it is not who we are.

As we progress in the book, we will look at ways we can begin undoing the grip the ego holds on us, but for now it is necessary that we understand four things:

1. The ego is not real.
2. The ego operates from fear.
3. The ego has no internal self-worth.
4. The ego needs external stimuli to validate itself.

THE EMPLOYEES' METHODS FOR COPING

Let's look at how employees, operating from their self-created egos, are currently coping with the politics, pain, and misery in businesses. The ego's strategies are created to avoid feeling fear and lack of self-worth.

IDENTIFICATION

Identification occurs because the ego has no authentic power, so it must create roles and identities that it believes are worthy. These false identities are like characters in a movie with certain characteristics that define their role in any situation. They rely on the drama to keep their false identity in place. Creating a lot of drama substantiates the identity or role, and continues to keep the ego alive.

Peace and quiet would cause the identity to dissolve, so the ego must keep the atmosphere stirred up by playing out these roles and dramatic episodes. The drama surrounding the ego is self-sustaining and persistent. The cause of the drama is unconscious, and therefore, it is hard to recognize the need for drama in oneself.

In addition, the complexity of the drama makes it difficult to discern the source and one's part in creating it. It has a certain momentum that tends to draw in other players, which then validates the chosen roles and keeps perpetuating the drama.

But under the drama, which is feeding on itself, is a huge *FEAR* of being exposed by each of the egos in the drama. This nagging fear ultimately depresses and exhausts the very players who originated the drama.

RESISTANCE

Resistance is the ego's attempt to keep in place the shields that prevent awareness of the fears and insecurities from coming to the surface. The belief system of the ego is actually so small that it cannot stand the challenge from a higher source. The ego is ever alert and vigilant to defend itself against anything it perceives as a threat. Whatever is resisted continues to persist and actually becomes even more powerful and vexing to the ego.

Resistance is really just a defense, but only the ego needs defending. When one is authentically strong, no defense is needed. A defensive posture in yourself or another is really a mask of fear. If you know this, you will begin to give up your own defenses and see past the defenses of others.

You can also begin to see that when you attack others or corner people in some way, you actually hook their ego so that they become more defensive. The more you push, the more the other ego will need to defend its position and prove itself to be right. What the ego believes it must defend is actually the very thing that would set the individual free.

Facing the denied fear beneath the defense is usually seen as insulting to the ego. Challenging the fear would lead to liberation. But the ego will project the fear onto another rather than look behind its own mask!

GRANDIOSITY

Grandiosity is the ego's shallow attempt to convince itself that it is powerful. It supports this belief with other people and uses external things to help validate this role or image it has created—an image it doesn't actually believe itself. This role the ego takes is also fraught with anxiety because of the ego's fear of being found out or exposed as a fraud.

The companion to grandiosity and self-boasting is pride. Pride, unlike authentic power, is demonstrating to others a sense of superiority or one-upmanship. The ego is truly very fragile and is always seeking ways to fortify itself, but fails to look within, where the only true power resides.

This ego technique seeks fame and personal glory to help elevate itself.

Authentic power needs no such claim, but often receives the recognition and admiration from others that the ego desires but cannot generate.

MANIPULATION

Manipulation is a technique employed by the ego in an attempt to control others, circumstances, and outcomes. This is based on the belief that the individual is not safe—therefore, the ego must calculatingly "use" or manipulate others to do and be what the ego needs in order to survive. This insidious form of control of others is often difficult to recognize, but is always felt by those being manipulated.

Manipulation is not an example of power, as the ego believes, but rather the opposite, a demonstration of weakness and fear of the future.

Control is seen as strength by the ego.

The other forms of control include structure and routine, and they give the ego a framework for feeling secure. However, it is a false sense of security.

The world of control and manipulation is like living in a very small house with tiny windows and doors, keeping people and opportunities out. It is a small world, lacking in spontaneity and freedom. It limits the authentic self from expanding, and keeps the ego in an artificial world of safety.

ALLIANCES

Alliances are ways the ego in the workplace joins with others to strengthen its position. Gossip and backbiting are attempts to briefly elevate the status of those engaged in it, but does so, at the cost of adding further negativity into the environment. The momentary sense of relief is usually followed by an unconscious sense of guilt.

Sometimes alliances can occur in what are described as political groups, bargaining groups, or any group of individuals joined together for the purpose of overcoming another group. They occur as a "cause"—usually with a mighty mission—but actually result in polarity of groups. A true armistice or resolution occurs when there is a reconciliation of ideas. It is not by a commitment to an unyielding position or stand that the ego demands.

This is not to be confused with taking a stand for or making a commitment to a valuable purpose or higher principle that contributes to the common good.

Aligning yourself with a universal principle is a way to enlightenment.

Aligning yourself with a group dedicated to the needs of a special interest to fulfill personal agendas is what's seen most often in the workplace.

The key is to ask yourself, "Who benefits from this alliance?" If it is for a special interest group, a select few trying to gain power, it is an alliance of the ego, trying to strengthen itself.

SABOTAGING

Sabotaging is a technique, employed by the ego in the workplace, to attempt to disempower others through an attack in some form on the person or persons perceived as a threat to the ego's identity.

Sabotaging comes in all forms, from the subtlest comments designed to cause doubt about the credibility of a person to out-and-out verbal, and occasionally, physical attacks.

This demonstration of the ego's power is really a substitute for the ego's lack of actual power.

Other examples of sabotage in the workplace are harassment and discrimination based on perceived differences, such as sexual preferences, gender, race, religion, economic groups, etc.

DIS-ASSOCIATION

Dis-association is the ego's final attempt to thwart any attack on its identity with the decision: "It's not me, it's them."

Therefore, the logical solution is to leave the workplace and find a more welcoming and accepting environment where the individual will be truly appreciated. However, since this technique is yet another outward projection of the problem with no change from within, the new environment will soon prove to be just as threatening and emotionally turbulent.

The new environment is often more intense. The drama escalates. The ego goes from a local stage to "Broadway Theater."

COSTS TO EMPLOYERS WHEN MANAGERS
DEPLETE THE ENERGY OF EMPLOYEES

Egos, masquerading as leaders throughout businesses everywhere, are costing companies immeasurable dollars. The damage that they inflict on the people they lead depletes the energy level, as well as the spirit and vitality of those people.

Countless young people enter the work force with enthusiasm, spirit, and fresh ideas to contribute to the organization. Then I see them gradually beaten down to soon become other egos, defending and pretending in an effort to survive with minimum damage.

Their inherent potential and talents are wasted. They begin looking around for another company or career, either because their family is complaining or because the doctor is ordering a change due to the stress they are experiencing.

What is the energy force or fuel that drives companies? Is it not the energy of its people?

This leak of energy and creative power goes unrecognized by businesses, as they analyze every other element of their operations to determine how to increase profitability, reduce costs, and increase productivity. It is as though someone is shooting holes in the gas tank and wondering why they are getting poor mileage.

It is time for leaders to recognize they are shooting themselves in the foot when they allow this ego-driven management, which is actually operating from fear, to continue.

Some ego-driven managers bring their people to their knees, and people on their knees are not very productive. Many companies would be better off eliminating many of the management positions and just allowing people to work on their own! Individuals would at least not be under the kind of pressure that wounds and depresses their very energy and life force.

The leadership style today is escalating its top-down, machine-like attitude. But people are not machines that can be simply plugged in and expected to work. The result of this pressure on people is not only the anguish by everyone, but the reduction of energy, productivity, and success of the company.

Employees do not feel loyal in this environment, nor can companies attract and retain employees with this atmosphere. The current leadership is unwittingly disempowering and damaging the core of its resources, which is the fuel driving the organization.

A sad repercussion of this destructive attitude is that it ultimately affects the quality of life in our country as dispirited people go home to their families in a state of exhaustion and distress.

One of the common complaints I hear from management is that it is hard to find good employees, and that many of the employees today are negative and unappreciative. This projection onto the employees solves nothing, and my question to those leaders or managers is: "Would the employees not be more positive in a happier environment? And aren't happy people more productive?"

Some ego-driven leaders acknowledge the possibility that this is true but still continue to want to be right in their complaints. It appears to be a Catch-22 or a chicken-or-the-egg situation.

But leadership will have to become accountable for the work environment, first. This will require understanding and then giving up this egotistical form of management currently operating in businesses today. In return, management will reap the rewards of a more successful business if they take on the change I am going to describe. If not, the suffering and political discord will continue to rise.

The current lack of trust and respect in the environment leads to dissatisfaction and discouragement by everyone involved. It is time to come face to face with this critical dilemma. It is an overdue journey.

We must begin practicing a new kind of leadership, a leadership that creates an environment of compassion.

Leaders need to address their own inadequacies and learn to become authentically strong rather than driven by their insatiable egos. Relationships need to be rebuilt, and genuine communication needs to become the basis of operating within organizations.

In the next chapter, we will look at what I call "enlightened leadership" and distinguish it from the ego-driven style currently in practice.

CHAPTER TWO

What Is Enlightened Leadership?

THE ENLIGHTENED LEADER

What does enlightened leadership look like?

True leadership is the process in which the spirit, within the leader, recognizes that same spiritual essence in those who are being led. This recognition automatically provides a conduit or channel of energy that propels everyone involved into the dedication and action necessary to achieve the vision or goal.

This approach to leadership is not being practiced in today's workplace. But if it were, it would make a significant difference in the work environment, as well as the way we conduct business.

What must be done to bring about this enlightened leadership?

It begins, first, with the leader. The leader directs the focus on characteristics and actions stemming from the ego and learns to gently remove these blocks. Remember that the ego prevents true leadership from being expressed. So when one works on challenging the needs of the ego, authentic power and spiritual essence are then being allowed to emerge.

Secondly, the leader must recognize and acknowledge this same power within each person in the group being led.

The powerful inner qualities of a leader are:

1. Vision
2. Trust
3. Honor
4. Commitment

5. Affinity
6. Defenselessness / Non-Resistance
7. Patience
8. Acceptance
9. Integrity
10. Compassion

Though the terminology may sound familiar, these qualities are not being practiced in today's business environment.

Until we see this change come about, the drama and pain in the workplace will continue to soar. When leadership can come from an open and trusting heart, we will begin to see the needed transformation.

This kind of leadership comes from a compassionate heart and cannot be feigned. The leader must be genuine, or the energy exchange between the leader and group members will not foster growth and inspiration.

Leading other people requires giving up personal goals in exchange for group decisions. It also includes seeing the brilliance and uniqueness in each individual. The level, reached in enlightened leadership, is determined by commitment and the willingness of the leader to give up the needs of the ego.

It is easier in theory than in practice because our egos are obstinate. Challenging the ego means:

- ◆ Giving up the need to know all the answers
- ◆ Giving up an attachment to the outcome
- ◆ Giving up the need to be superior
- ◆ Being able to be wrong
- ◆ Listening instead of talking

The ego does not do any of the above well, and therefore blocks the free flow of creative energy that comes from the group process.

The unenlightened leader has a difficult time seeing that the ego is identifying with the results and that it has a predetermined outcome. The ego-driven leader does not see that the imaginative input that comes from the group process will be missing if the leader has the ending already defined.

Ego-driven leaders believe the vision and goals are something to be imparted to the group and then, somehow, as "excellent leaders," they can convince and persuade the team to share or "buy into" it. This is the misperception of the ego and is the biggest obstacle to teamwork.

THE IMPOSTER SYNDROME—IDENTIFYING EIGHT EGO-DRIVEN LEADERS

In order to identify the powerful qualities of an enlightened leader, it is helpful to look at some common roles and actions demonstrated by the ego-driven leader. In contrast to the powerful abilities of an enlightened leader to promote creativity, to energize, and to incite action through honor and respect of those being led, the ego-driven manager *operates from fear.*

The enlightened leader creates an environment of synergism in which all members of a group align with a higher purpose, and together develop a passion and commitment to achieve the goal. The ego-driven leader does not.

This positive group dynamic in the enlightened leader's workplace occurs quite naturally, when the barriers of the ego are not blocking the flow of energy.

Ego-driven leaders, in their effort to strengthen their illusion of themselves, create ego "static" or interference of free flowing ideas in the workplace. This interference affects those who are being led.

Let's look carefully at the qualities of the leader who is operating from this ego thought system. This leader, who actually does have many talents and abilities, does not really believe this. Ego-driven leaders have incredible doubts and fears. They are relying on their self-created ego rather than their inner strength, power, and wisdom that are available when they are aligned with spirit.

Deep down inside, ego-driven leaders do not believe they are worthy of the title or position they hold! This belief leads to the unbearable fear that the truth will be discovered and that it will be exposed that they, indeed, are imposters. This "Imposter Syndrome" is so prevalent that it has become the norm. It has become the current model of management.

What does the ego-driven leader do, then, to protect this secret?

Like all the egos in the workplace, ego-driven leaders have certain techniques to ensure their position and so-called security. It is especially harmful in the workplace, when there are leaders operating at this level, because of their perceived power. It is very difficult to challenge or not be controlled by these techniques if you are one of those being led.

The following techniques are used by the ego to cast itself as a leader. Most of these roles are actually recognized by people in the group. But because of the perceived power of the leaders and the perceived weakness of those being led, it is rarely addressed.

These techniques are unconscious to those using them since the techniques do provide a sense of power—"false power" to the egos that are playing these roles. Like all things created by the ego thought system, however, this sense of power is temporary as *fear* lurks beneath the surface.

THE DICTATOR / BULLY

This ego-driven leader uses intimidation and fear to get people to do what the ego believes is needed to accomplish goals. The ego has a hidden motive as well: validation that it is the all-powerful.

This false leader has no ability to feel compassion or understanding of others. The ego's need to strengthen its small image of itself precludes any awareness of others or the willingness to look outside itself. The ego's greatest fear in this role is that it will be discovered that it is powerless.

STAR-OF-THE-TEAM LEADER / KNOW-IT-ALL LEADER

This role allows the ego to stay in place by creating the appearance of being the champion, the rescuer of those less capable. This person has to be right because it maintains the ego's sense of superiority, which is believed to be necessary in being a leader.

Ironically, knowing everything prevents this leader from learning anything and blocks all flowing creativity from those being led. The ego's greatest fear is that one of the ones being led may actually be the understudy, waiting to replace the leader. But since the leader already knows everything, the employees cannot contribute anything anyway.

THE FAULT-FINDING / BLAMING LEADER

The technique employed by this ego-driven leader is an attempt to direct attention away from itself, so that the ego's actual fear and doubt will not be exposed.

Putting those being led in a defensive posture, by always looking for what is wrong, stifles any creativity and confidence in those who might otherwise contribute in an outstanding manner. The employee's focus becomes trying not to make a mistake, rather than working positively and productively.

THE DISCOUNTING LEADER

This method is employed to render those being led as impotent and inferior. Rather than acknowledge and praise those being led, ego-driven leaders use their people to elevate and strengthen what their own egos believe is their power position.

These ego-driven leaders rarely give others credit due them because that would threaten their position. The ego finds the weak are less intimidating to its own fragile sense of power. The employees never feel appreciated and begin feeling apathy toward any purposeful activity.

THE EMPIRE-BUILDER LEADER

Gaining territorial, political, financial, or a competitive advantage over others is the method this ego-driven leader uses to ensure the false image of power, which is actually a demonstration of a deep lack of worth. The deeper the sense of worthlessness, the larger the empire is needed to demonstrate the false power.

This ego is never satisfied and will continue to attempt to build a greater empire. But it is an endless, fruitless endeavor. The acquisition of symbols of power is the driving force behind this ego-driven leader.

THE PATRONIZING / PLACATING LEADER

Coming from a desperate fear of not being admired or needed, this leader appears, at first, to be compassionate and caring. The leader seems to agree and provide positive communication. But it is only when the action is not commensurate with the words that the lack of authenticity is demonstrated.

This ego-driven leader actually believes it has no power and therefore cannot step up to the plate, except in a subversive manner. This leader instills no confidence, respect, or trust on the part of the employees.

THE MICRO-MANAGER LEADER

This leader is the fearful ego that maintains all sense of identity and security by controlling the situation and others in it. To prevent anything from going "wrong" and the ego being held accountable, this leader uses a microscopic vigilance over people and events of the day.

The people being led feel like they are being held in a cage, allowed to move but only in a tiny arena. Ego-driven leaders are afraid of losing face and believe that this high control will keep them safe.

THE MARTYR / RIGHTEOUS LEADER

This role requires the ego-driven leader to appear as benevolent and very righteous. This leader has the best interests of everyone at heart, but there are too many conditions over which he or she has no control. This leader is fearful of taking a stand, and instead feels himself or herself to be a victim of circumstances or conditions.

This ego works relentlessly, putting in endless hours, which demonstrate its dedication. No one can keep up with this one, so employees feel guilty and believe they have to demonstrate this same workaholism to keep their jobs.

These examples of various ego methods of leadership are not all inclusive. Variations and overlapping do occur. It is important to understand that these roles are not taken consciously. They are simply the ego's way of coping in the environment where fear and insecurity are present.

The tragedy is that these ego-defined roles compound the pain and suffering for everyone with whom they come in contact.

Recognizing these various roles is usually fairly easy when looking at others. The difficulty and denial arises in seeing them in one's self. Denial is a powerful technique to avoid dealing with the ego's dysfunctional issues, methods, and actions. It takes unrelenting commitment to the goal of transformation to overcome the denial that seeks to keep the ego in place.

Beneath the surface of a leader's ego is the fear that one or more of those being led, in actuality, would rather sabotage or undermine the rule of the leader and his ideas. This fear impacts the leader by reinforcing the ego's need for creating a further sense of defensiveness, which, of course, is a barrier to synergism and group will. This underlying fear of the employees renders the leader impotent.

This mask of overt confidence that the leader wears is a hindrance to the process and prevents opportunities for group expansion and purpose. But the leader is almost always unaware that it is a disguise because the ego is so crafty.

The ego continues its attempts to validate itself at the expense of others, giving itself the illusion of authority. So discovering the source of the fear and releasing that fear are goals of this book.

TRUE ALIGNMENT

True alignment brings about a new vision that creates enthusiasm and clear direction for everyone. An enlightened leader reaches beyond the low expectations of the ego, and helps release the full potential and spirit of those in the group. This can only occur in a trusting and respectful environment, where equality and affinity for one another are present.

Purposeful action is only attained when the goal is worthy of the energy expelled to achieve it. So much of the activity in the workplace is inefficient, misdirected, and unfulfilling. The ego in the workplace often spends endless time on mindless activities and trivia that do not satisfy the soul or spirit in one's self.

Meetings and activities in the workplace are often a waste of time, acting like a gigantic procrastination game, preventing people from experiencing the real intention of work and of life. The valid game of life is discovering the inner self and its power to create.

Everyone has talents and gifts meant to be expressed, which results in inner personal satisfaction and joy. This is the true labor of love, the rewarding experience of contributing and creating from one's authentic self. This labor of love is demonstrated in the work of artists, authors, composers, dancers, and anyone who is expressing from one's true being.

Individuals in any organization have the potential to contribute from that inner source and wellspring of creativity, but unfortunately it is stifled in most organizations because of the power struggles and conflicting attitudes and activities occurring everyday.

All the mindless and mechanical activity experienced by the ego in the workplace is wasted time for the company, and it is a tragedy in terms of the individual's satisfaction and spiritual evolution.

An environment, not providing opportunities for meaningful expression of oneself and one's abilities, adds to the waylaid journey of discovery to the inner greatness in each of us. Individuals become lethargic, dispirited, and depressed rather than invigorated and inspired. Energy is used to fight the battles and resist the attacks, rather than pursuing new levels of achievement and new possibilities for business success.

Tim, a thirty-eight-year-old husband and father, was a manager with a large computer consulting firm. He held two degrees and had immense experience in both the technical area and the business arena. When I first met Tim, I was impressed with his confidence and creativity. In addition to his business acumen, he also had great marketing skills. He was outgoing and a good networker in the community. He was a good public speaker, and often spoke to various associations and meeting groups. His enthusiasm and high energy were very remarkable.

A year later, I saw Tim and he seemed dramatically different. He was quiet. His usual sense of humor was sadly absent. As I worked with his company, he seemed reticent to contribute. I even began wondering if I had offended him in some way. A couple months later, he announced he was leaving the firm. I finally talked with him and discovered the source of the problem.

A new senior partner had taken over Tim's department and had redefined the goals of the division. This senior partner was Tim's boss for the past year, and he managed his people in a highly critical manner. He was the classical Fault-Finding / Blaming Leader, always looking for mistakes with everyone's work.

He thought he was helping his team by pointing out what they were doing wrong. This management style was his attempt to push and generate a high level of production in his people, but the process was intimidating and energy-deflating to those being led.

All those being managed under this ego-driven leadership style began looking over their shoulders and spending most of their time worrying about making mistakes, rather than finding new ways of increasing the business opportunities.

Tim had become extremely dispirited. As a result, his actual production had gone down. His once effervescent personality had changed to one of quiet desperation and discouragement. Tim finally found a position with another organization after his doctor warned him about his high blood pressure and his wife became concerned about his depression. Unfortunately, Tim had suffered immense pressure and strain for almost a year before leaving. So the company lost an outstanding employee and never knew why.

This sad scenario occurs quite often as managers fail to provide an environment that brings out the best in people. Businesses inadvertently reduce the success of the company; but more importantly, they cause undue hardship and emotional anxiety for those who work under their managers.

Other owners or managers in the company are often ignorant of the lack of compassion of a particular partner or manager. They are unaware that another manager is causing so much confusion that results in loss of productivity and even employees. And employees rarely tell management about their concerns or complaints because they fear recrimination.

Leaders, who are not aware that they are operating from the ego, continue creating this unstable environment. Siding with the ego is actually an attempt to circumvent and avoid the inevitable journey of waking up from the drama in the workplace.

The path to spirit is everyone's ultimate destiny. Some people are actively pursuing the journey, some are stumbling on obstacles and tripping their way through it, and others are actively resisting it. Many people would actually rather remain numb and not do the work it takes to come out of the drama.

For some, the fear of the unknown is even more threatening than the current situation. Therefore, these individuals choose to remain a victim in the muddle of politics and opinions, rather than face the real conflict—the conflict with the ego self. When this is the leader or manager, it is very detrimental to the workplace.

If leaders of the group begin recognizing the traps of their own egos, the leaders can then begin to bring about a remarkable change for those being led. Leaders will discover ways to better guide the group process so that the flow continues, unhampered by the constraints of their own egos as well as by the constraints of the egos in the group.

Teamwork relies on the leader, transcending the immense needs of the ego and operating from inner power, allowing others to contribute from their vibrant and powerful source. This kind of alignment creates a potent opportunity for the common good of the organization.

A CLOSER LOOK AT THE QUALITIES OF ENLIGHTENED LEADERSHIP

The emergence of the qualities of enlightened leadership comes through the process of identifying and removing the obstacles created by the relentless ego.

The ego cannot practice the qualities of leadership that I am describing because the ego is only an actor.

True leadership comes from the higher self.

Let's look more closely at the qualities of enlightened leadership:

VISION

Vision is the ability to see an expanded possibility or mental picture in the future from an elevated viewpoint in the present.

This picture stretches the imagination, stirs the emotions, and inspires others to action and commitment. It acknowledges the creative force and potential of each individual as necessary to the attainment of the vision.

Holding a clear image, the leader is not deterred by present circumstances or obstacles but sees the vision as a future certainty.

TRUST

Trust is the reliance on the spiritual group process, rather than individual or personal goals. It is recognizing the contribution and participation of each individual as a necessary component. Trust is belief in each person without judgment, restriction, or control. Trust in others helps them soar to new heights.

HONOR

Honor is acknowledging the spirit in everyone. It is the respect and faith in others as the powerful and creative beings that they are. Honor is seeing in others what they sometimes cannot see in themselves.

COMMITMENT

Commitment is giving one's word with an unswerving promise to fulfill it. It is a freely given pledge, coming from authentic power—not from an obligation, not from lack of freedom. It is dedication and follow-through on that which one has chosen.

AFFINITY

Affinity is a genuine and sincere caring for and appreciation of others. Affinity sees others as the self and understands "we are all one." Affinity sees the connection and relationship of all people and has gratitude for others. One who has true affinity for others does not judge or harm others.

DEFENSELESSNESS / NON-RESISTANCE

Defenselessness / Non-Resistance is the recognition that there is nothing to defend. Only the ego needs a defense to protect itself from facing the fears it does not want exposed. Defending and resisting are sure signs that the ego is in charge. Defenselessness and non-resistance are qualities of authentic strength.

PATIENCE

Patience is the knowledge that there is a time and a season for all things. Patience trusts in a greater scheme, and is not attached to the outcome or the timing. Patience is being content with not knowing, and waiting does not cause anxiety or doubt. Patience is given to the self and to those being led.

ACCEPTANCE

Acceptance is the recognition that we are all equal and that we originate from the same source. There are no differences in reality. Acceptance does not distinguish others on the basis of religion, race, gender, economic status, or any other conditions. Acceptance extends understanding, not separation.

INTEGRITY

Integrity is wholeness and consistency. Integrity is unwavering and steadfast. Integrit does not bend and is not shaped by outside influences, but it stands strong in the face of temptation. A person with integrity can always be trusted.

COMPASSION

Compassion sees the world from another's point of view. Compassion is not sympathy; it is knowing another's heart as one's own. It is having deep regard for another's feelings and welfare. True compassion is extended to all people and always brings gentle support.

These inner qualities of true leadership cannot be learned. They must be a result of courageously giving up the demands of the tenacious ego. This relinquishment, however, is not effortless because the ego has been in control for so long.

The world is currently operating from the perspective of power from external factors. But authentic power cannot be bought, acquired, learned, or even emulated. It must arise from the inner core of one's being, the true self. It can then never be taken away.

Nothing can extinguish the joy and peace of your inner greatness. This power will allow you to fulfill your heart's deepest desire, which is one's purpose in life. And as a leader, you will help others reach this same possibility.

THE TEAM AS WE KNOW IT AND THE
BREAKDOWN OF LEADERSHIP

Today's businesses recognize that teamwork is desirable for creating and meeting goals for the organization. But the ego-driven business leaders today are not aware that the alignment of the team is dependent on the participation of all team members. They try to "sell" the vision to the employees.

Since the vision has no meaning for the employees, it is impossible to create genuine motivation within the employees to pursue the goals.

CEOs, presidents, and managers complain that the employees are not committed to the company's vision and goals. Or worse yet, the company either has no mission or it exists simply in their own minds.

Frequently, employees have no idea what the mission is. So how could they possibly be committed to it?

Leaders also grumble that employees do not work hard enough and are not loyal. They say it's hard to get good employees, fully projecting the problem on the people rather than looking at themselves.

There are three reasons for these problems:

1. The employees have no input or participation in the goal-setting process.
2. The goals only serve the owners or upper management.
3. Even when employees have input, the underlying power struggles between people prevent the individuals from working as a team.

This is much like a family attempting to plan a vacation. If the children are not involved in the decisions, it is difficult to convince them that it is a desirable destination. The children didn't get to help choose and have input; therefore, they will likely be resistant to the trip itself. They want to go to Disneyland, for example, and the trip is planned for visiting Aunt Martha and the Smithsonian.

Planning together will bring forth goals and activities to which everyone can commit. It becomes an exciting and enjoyable plan.

Planning the family vacation together, you will find the children helping in every way to make the trip a success. They will generate ideas for finding someone to care for the yard, take the pets, bring in the mail, and even pack their own clothes. Their inner enthusiasm will produce energy and motivation to carry out the necessary actions for the vacation and make it fun for everyone.

Ego-driven leaders do not understand this process. They are afraid to take their hands off the wheel, believing they must be in control of the vehicle.

The ego is fearful of losing control because the ego believes it must direct the outcome. This very attitude is what prevents the full spectrum of creativity and passion to be expressed when a group comes together.

Ego-driven leaders cast themselves in a role that is superior to others, rather than acknowledging the same spiritual essence in everyone in the group. The need to be greater than others restricts, if not blocks, the contribution from others. The synergistic power and ingenuity that comes from alignment and working toward a common goal are unavailable to the group.

When people are denied freedom of expression, power struggles result. These internal battles become one more block in the free exchange of energy. The breakdown of the leadership becomes the collapse of the team.

An egotistical leader hooks the egos of the members of the group. Many feel they must challenge the leader. Individuals then blame one another for the lack of desired progress. Teams become a battleground or a stalemate, rather than a progressive opportunity for moving the company forward.

In summary, this book is designed to help identify the drama that is being played out in businesses throughout the country and to teach people how to unhook from the reactions and counter-reactions of egos in the workplace.

It is most detrimental when egos are in the role of leadership. But that is also the place to begin unraveling the complex entanglement of egos. It starts with the leaders, having the responsibility of facing their own challenges and working toward internal transformation.

True leaders can release those they lead by allowing them the freedom and opportunity to become restored to their true identities, just as the leaders have to come to know themselves.

CHAPTER THREE

The Stage and the Passionate Drama in the Workplace

THE WORKPLACE AS A STAGE

John and I emerged from the theater among a happy crowd of people who had clearly enjoyed the movie we had just seen.

This particular movie appealed to both genders and had many interesting characters, struggling with various universal themes. One moment we were brought to tears and the next, elevated to laughter. We cheered as the hero won his battle, suffered when a main character died, and rejoiced when true love conquered all.

I said, referring to one of the characters in the movie, "What about Robert? What will become of him now that everyone else left? "

John answered wisely, "Robert is getting his just dessert. It's justice being played out."

Then we looked at each other and laughed.

For a moment, even after leaving the theater, we had forgotten it was only a movie.

Robert is just a role—played by an actor. For a few seconds, however, we were so drawn into this movie that we had forgotten that it was not real. We felt the emotions as though we were actually a part of the drama.

The human dynamics and emotional drama in the workplace are much like those interactions and drama we see in the theater. However, this drama in the workplace is causing real emotional problems and physical symptoms, due to the stress of working in a turbulent environment.

People everywhere are experiencing profound discontent in their occupations and careers. They are feeling exhausted by the ever-growing psychological dysfunction in the workplace.

How can we bring a clearer perception to this drama?

Let's look at the following comparison as a model for understanding the current workplace:

THE STAGE

An actor needs a stage. He then needs a compelling drama in which he can create his character and play out the scenes with passion. He also needs other actors and actresses to be cast in the drama—characters whom he can challenge, compete with, and overcome; characters who support his drama of victory, defeat, love, loss, and even death.

The ego is also an actor, a false identity playing a role that we believe is real. Its stage is the workplace, and its drama is a tragedy—complete with pain, suffering, triumph, and loss.

This tragedy is a real-life tragedy as long as we exist here on the physical plane. We cannot go home and be thankful it was only a movie or stage play.

It is our life.

When we view the workplace as the stage where a drama is being played out, we can see that it has all the components of any play or movie that we might go and see for entertainment. This can be very useful in bringing insight to the source of our anguish in the workplace.

First, however, we must look at how the ego developed and became the actor that it is.

Secondly, we need to look at the elements of literary drama, the elements that we see in a theater production or a movie we attend. With these elements, we will then see how drama is occurring daily on the stage of the workplace.

This comparison to a literary drama can turn the spotlight on the destructive human dynamics occurring in businesses today. It can help you begin to see a way out of a reoccurring tragedy.

It will take courage to challenge your own ego, and certainly more courage to challenge the dramatic role you are playing in real life on the stage that we know as the workplace.

THE EGO—A SELF-CREATED ACTOR

The ego is the image we have come to believe of who we are. It is not "bad" and, in fact, we could not function on the planet without an ego. The ego personality is necessary, just as our body is needed, to navigate through life.

It is like a costume or role that we play, which functions for us in various situations. We send out an actor in our place—a proxy—an inadequate, small version of ourselves. Then, we complain about the performance.

The problem occurs because we are disconnected from the eternal, spiritual source and rely only on the ego to operate in the world. The ego is only a portion of who we really are.

The ego bases its identity on external validation and operates from fear. This fear is a result of not feeling connected to our inner spirit. When we are in fear, we can be sure we are operating from the ego.

The ego does not rely on authentic power but seeks it outside itself. The ego wants to protect its secret—that it is powerless. So it creates an identity.

The ego is an actor. It wears a mask so that others cannot see that we do not know who we are. If we recognized our inner spiritual greatness, our ego would not have to work so hard acting out a role to convince ourselves and others that we are valuable.

The ego first begins its development at some time in early childhood when the innocent and free little child discovered that just "being" is not enough in the physical world. The child begins developing a concept of who he/she is, mainly from the influences and interactions of family and friends. The child learns to define its identity based on external feedback.

Positive reactions from family and friends support the child's identity as it develops. This identity or beginning of the self-created ego then gets further reinforcement from the outside world as it continues in life. Identity grows stronger.

For example, "She's such a smart little girl" or "He's such a strong little boy" motivates the child to continue exhibiting behavior that elicits this positive response. The world continues to impact the child's decision to be an "identity." This conditioning process and labeling from others strengthens the self-created role.

Somewhere along the way, some kind of pain occurs. So the child makes an unconscious decision to create a way of being able to cope with future pains and situations that will be encountered. The painful experience could be anything from a reprimand to a full-scale attack by someone who begins the protective process, but the child begins to create another portion of the ego identity to ensure safety and to defend the ego from fear of pain or loss of love.

The more negativity the child encounters, the stronger the need to build up defenses and rely on the ego identity to protect itself. The child begins a life-long process of pretending to be that which gets positive reinforcement and therefore, strengthening the ego, and building defenses against that which is perceived as fearful or threatening. This *pretending and defending* becomes the identity and way of being for the child on into adulthood.

Even our educational process shapes and conditions children for coping and achieving in school. The research for my master's thesis on self-esteem in education revealed that children are labeled throughout school.

For example, the round robin reading groups in which children learn to read are based on reading levels or abilities to read. This creates stigmas. And children all know by the second grade, at the latest, which is the high, middle, and low group.

Children then compensate in other ways if they don't feel validation for their efforts in one area. Unfortunately, they often feel a lack of confidence in other areas due to the labeling in one, such as a reading group level. The insecurity that the ego is trying to protect, the fear of being unworthy, is often reinforced in school, because of its competitive nature.

The power of that kind of "labeling" is demonstrated when my adult audiences are visibly relieved to hear there is no correlation between intelligence and the ability to spell. They have often held throughout their lives that message of "you can't spell" as a sign they are inadequate and not very bright.

So all kinds of methods for survival and protection are developed as a part of the identity. With time, the ego identity becomes so strong that the individual believes that is really who she or he is.

The ego, as an actor, is a made-up identity that has no sense of internal worth and must, therefore, create its self-worth from the outside. To cover this fear of being exposed as fake, the ego has many methods to validate itself from external sources.

These outside symbols of power are designed to convince the ego and others that it is very powerful. But all attempts to support this facade are simply cover ups of the actual doubt and insecurity the ego experiences. The ego is not connected to its true source or authentic inner self.

If you don't believe that the ego relies on externals to validate itself and reinforce its identity, ask yourself any or all of the following questions:

- Who would I be if I were not someone's father, mother, brother, sister, husband, wife, boyfriend, girlfriend, child, etc.?
- Who would I be if I did not have this position, title, or role in my job?
- Who would I be if I suddenly had no money?
- Who would I be if I had no home?
- What does my choice of automobile say about me?
- What do my choices of clothes and hairstyle say about me?
- Who would I be if I belonged to no organizations?
- What do my choices of jewelry, toys, sports teams, recreational sports, and entertainment activities say about me?

- Who would I be if I did not live in this community, region, and country?
- What does my choice of music, television programs, and books say about me?
- Who would I be without my social groups and friends?
- Who would I be if I were never invited to anything, i.e. parties, weddings, events?
- Who would I be if I had no heritage?
- Who would I be if I had no church or religion?
- Who would I be if I had no name (or nobody knew my name)?
- Who would I be if I had no education or degrees?

Not all these questions apply to everyone, but most of us get much of our identity from the external links that are or have been a part of our lives.

But the spirit within us is greater than all the external definitions and connections we have that we believe substantiate us. Our soul is connected to all others on a much deeper level.

On a less spiritual level, we use others to carry out our drama and to define who we are. The many objects, titles, teams, social groups, affiliations, and money are simply symbols to show that we are worthy. They have no intrinsic value—only that which we assign them.

The ego is never at rest because it requires time and energy to play out the role it has designed for itself. It is also dependent on convincing others of its validity. It must stir up drama to keep reinforcing itself. This takes energy.

The ego is also on guard because it might be caught doing something that would expose itself to be a fraud. It must be ever alert. The anxiety, produced from this acting, causes the ego to be uptight most of the time, unable to give up its ever-watchful position.

Some of the ways you can recognize when the ego is operating instead of your real or authentic self is doing any of the following behaviors:

- Defending
- Attempting to be superior
- Controlling others or situations
- Creating drama
- Gossiping
- Blaming and attacking
- Claiming to be right
- Creating enemies
- Rejecting others
- Avoiding accountability
- Boasting
- Interrupting
- Feigning benevolence
- Being self-righteous
- Being the victim
- Addictive behavior
- Being the first to speak
- Having the last word
- Denial of any of the above

The ego has a primary drive to create, within itself and toward others, a sense of superiority. This "one-upmanship" is permeating the ego world. It is based on the false belief that if "I'm smarter, richer, prettier, nicer," or in any number of ways superior, then "you can't hurt me or make me small."

However, creating this feeling of superiority requires a lot of attention and constant vigilance, which is exhausting. And worst of all, it produces exactly the opposite result desired—it alienates others.

But the temporary "fix" that the ego receives for appearing superior and having authority over others is very strong. It produces a powerful surge that reinforces the ego's need for supremacy, but, of course, the fix is only temporary.

The ego's plan for sustaining itself is a complex matter, lying beneath the surface but needing constant attention. The gigantic "play" and its interactions are going on worldwide and are so believable that breaking out or through the enormous illusion is terribly difficult.

It usually takes a crisis, a lot of pain, or a situation to temporarily "wake" a person up. These moments, when they do occur, can lead to freedom from the ego, if one chooses it. Even then, it is rare that a person can achieve it for a long period of time. So powerful is the collective consciousness.

Misery and discontent have reached huge proportions in today's workplace. The need has never been greater for a way to end the despair and agony, even though, in many cases, it is not being acknowledged. So great is the denial of the ego.

Yet, as a consultant, I have watched people break down and cry as they describe their life at work.

Using the model of a theater or movie drama can help break through this clouded vision and chaos. One by one, as people wake up and begin seeing a new, freer way to live in peace and harmony, stemming from the powerful inner self, a change of consciousness will occur.

First, it will happen within individuals, then in the collective consciousness. Finally, this change in consciousness will impact the world and how we experience it.

THE ELEMENTS OF THE DRAMA
IN THE WORKPLACE

Understanding the drama and its components requires seeing that your ego is an actor playing out its drama with passion and conviction, believing it all to be real. The drama is the emotional turbulence created in this ever-escalating play of human beings suffering with each other on this "workplace" stage.

The drama intensifies as the characters react and counter-react to one another. The interactions cause emotional pain. But what the ego doesn't understand is that the pain is self-created within each individual, based on past experiences.

Your ego believes the other characters cause your emotions and responses. What is actually happening is that you are reliving past "scenes" originated in childhood, whenever your ego is hooked by another ego. You then act out a response, based on a role from the conditioning your ego received early in its development.

So we could say, little children are actually the ones playing out the dramas and running the businesses of the world as well as our governments!

Let's take a close look at the various elements of a literary drama and see how they apply to the workplace:

THEME OF THE EGO

The ego's true theme is "I am not worthy."

It must cover its shameful secret with tactics and strategies to convince itself and others that it is real. Its greatest fear is that it will be exposed as only an actor. So it creates an identity that will give the ego a sense that it is powerful, although it is false power.

We will later look at how each individual develops a theme, based on experiences from the past, and we will learn how it has been running our lives.

STAR / PROTAGONIST

This is the ego, casting you as the hero or heroine of the drama.

However, each ego in the workplace perceives itself to be the star, so the difficulty occurs when other characters do not play out their roles as cast by your ego. Being the star of your drama keeps your focus on you, while the other characters on the stage do not know they are cast as bit players or minor characters in your show. They believe they are the stars of their own drama.

Your starring role will lead you to act out your theme, plot, and motives. It is so unconscious, though, that you won't even recognize that you played this performance before.

SCRIPT

Your script has been written by your ego and makes perfect sense to you. Most of your lines have been memorized from years of repetition in similar scenes on different stages.

Again, the confusion and lack of communication comes about when the other players do not have your script. They don't know their lines as assigned by you.

PLOT

The plot is the story line or action that occurs and is motivated by each individual ego's motives. The motives are unconscious, but they are designed to get a response from the other players, which will satisfy your ego's need to relive the past.

But of course, this required and expected response doesn't happen exactly the way you want, so the plot thickens and the drama intensifies. An actor may change stages, but the plot never varies until the source of the drama is exposed.

MOTIVES

Motives are the unconscious goals and expectations of the ego, based on its experiences from the past.

Your ego will always find evidence to support its story line and will take you down the path to the consequences its plot demands, even if it is painful or disappointing on a conscious level. The ego would rather be right than happy.

Because we are unaware of our motives, it is difficult to change the action of the drama, so we continue to play it out in the same fashion.

We may begin to start wondering, "Why does this always happen to me?" or "This isn't fair. Why are people so _____?" You may fill in the blank because the belief system for each individual is unique and we see the world in our own fashion based on our perception and past experiences.

DIRECTOR

This, of course, is also the ego. Since the ego created the plot and cast the characters, based on its own motives from the past, only the ego could direct such a drama. The ego is the only one who knows the desired ending.

The director is usually experienced as a "voice" instructing the "star" how to carry out the role with adequate passion, pain, or heart-felt emotion. The goal of the director is to help the ego turn in an Academy Award winning performance.

The director knows what worked in the past in scenes of passion, pain, and suffering and the director will continue to direct the actor to carry out this same performance.

The director actually knows of no other way to do the acting other than from the past experiences with other characters that had similar roles.

CAMERA

Judgment is the automatic viewpoint, the lens and filter of the camera through which we see the drama in the workplace. It is based on a limited view from our small corner of the world. It is our viewpoint from our starring role. It is ours alone.

Other actors have their own cameras and filters, and they do not see the drama in any other way but their own. Herein lies the problem: The other actors do not play out the roles in which we cast them *based on our judgment*. They have their own scripts.

However, it gets very complex because we will usually still hear what we want to hear from the other characters because our expectation is so strong that it filters out other responses. We hear their lines the way our judgment perceives them, even though it is through a very clouded and distorted lens.

Judgment is so pervasive in the workplace and in the world that we don't even realize that we are doing it every moment of the day.

ACTION

The action occurs each day as the ego enters the stage and carries out its plot. The ego's driving force is "control" so it will expend incredible energy attempting to control self, others, and situations, believing this will keep it protected and its secret safe.

The action is exhausting because it is being motivated by fear and trepidation.

It is like a gigantic "chess game" of moving, waiting, watching, and being ever vigilant of the fearful claim, "Checkmate!"

ENEMY / ANTAGONIST

No play would be complete without the role of at least one enemy; there are usually several.

The enemies provide varying degrees of intensity in the drama. The enemy is different for different characters, based on their perceived threat to your ego. So the casting of the enemies are based on the ones who could hurt, expose, or overcome your ego. This can and does change throughout the drama, depending on the one who is perceived to be the most threatening.

Your ego, believing the enemy to be the source of its pain or envy, carries out a battle to overcome or prevent being overcome. This battle usually causes very strong emotions.

The interesting feature is that the enemy has appeared in other dramas with you but the face was different. The enemy continues to be unrecognized by your ego as the same enemy it has battled in the past.

CONSPIRACY

This is part of the story line in the plot that brings characters together for a single purpose: that of supporting each other's false identities.

These alliances are attempts to give the ego fortification and convince yourselves that all of you are strong by providing and gaining secret support. These alliances are based on personal agendas, not authentic caring for one another.

But having a common enemy creates a strong bond with others who are afraid of the same enemy. In the workplace, this is usually called "politics" or, more aptly, "gossip." The bond is false and will break easily as scenes change and different characters enter the stage.

THE CONFLICT

The star or main character of the drama has a conflict to resolve or overcome.

Throughout the play, the star believes the conflict is with the other characters, particularly the people cast as the enemies. This belief is a great misperception of the ego and it keeps you isolated and blind to the truth, the truth being that ALL BATTLES ARE WITH THE SELF.

THE CLIMAX

This is the high point in the drama when the emotion has reached its peak. It is at this point that the ego must make a decision. It is a critical choice and has the possibility of changing the direction of the drama.

The decision is always between two options: (1) "Should I follow the familiar path of pain and suffering offered by the ego?" or (2) "Should I choose the path of spirit, which leads to authentic power?"

The ego is tenacious and wants you to follow its road of never-ending misery. You are so deeply ingrained in your ego's way that choosing spirit over ego causes an enormous conflict.

Most often, you follow the well-worn path of the ego. The ego then leads you into another drama, often on a different stage with the same past.

The plot never varies, nor do the motives. All of them stem from the ego's past. Therefore, the drama is recreated but the outcome remains the same. Only the names and faces change on a new stage of endless episodes of your continuing drama.

Not until the ego finally surrenders can the authentic, spiritual self emerge to reclaim the present. Then only and only then is the ego freed from the self-imposed prison of an on-going "soap opera."

I believe this model of the "theater" can help dispel some of the misunderstandings and confusion in the current environment. It can give you a new picture of what is actually occurring by illuminating the source of the pain.

As you see that your ego is directing this drama and it will never lead you to a happy ending, you will then be ready to see a new view . . . looking behind the mask of the ego.

First, we must admit and concede that there is a tragedy in businesses today. This drama is not only detrimental to business success but, more importantly, to the very health and vitality of the people within the businesses.

Secondly, we must make a decision to be accountable and responsible for our own drama and start to extricate ourselves from it. It means making the necessary changes by committing to take purposeful action.

Are you willing to recognize the blocks thrown out by your ego? Are you willing to look within?

When you are, you will discover a new, calm way of responding from your inner spirit. You will no longer feel like a puppet on a stage, dependent on others for your identity and purpose. This is where true inner peace lies.

To accomplish this worthwhile journey you will need to practice challenging the ego's drama. This takes conscious attention and a commitment to yourself.

THE ENTANGLEMENT OF EGOS IN THE DRAMA

What does this entanglement of egos that carry out this on-going drama do to the workplace?

The suffering continues to grow. The play-acting goes on. It is all so difficult to discern.

Leaders, operating from the false sense of power from the drama and structure of today's workplace stage, inflict incredible harm to the employees and their ability to perform. The corporate structure or any other organizational system, that places people above and below one another, has the potential for causing people to be submissive, based on their being inferior.

Those leading from the ego are rarely aware of how destructive their tactics are, when they do not honor the equality and spirit within everyone. It is emotionally grueling for people at all levels. But it is particularly difficult for those being led because of their need for security in the job.

Bringing people to their knees is happening everywhere. No one can work productively, expansively, and creatively on his or her knees.

This false perception of power is occurring at all levels of management. It gives the ego-driven leader a temporary feeling of supremacy and perceived power. But the cost to the organization is immense, actually immeasurable. It is so rampant that those being led simply suffer, and then play out their own ego dramas—the dramas of victimization and pain.

Change in the drama and the restoration of people to their true identities are essential to bring about the peace and satisfaction that everyone desires.

But, as I have said, because of the perceived power of the leaders, they are the ones who must begin the process. The need for approval and security, by the employees from their employers, makes it almost impossible for the employees to initiate the change of unscrambling the drama themselves.

People have been describing to me the workplace as an almost impenetrable system of management that is creating difficult politics, indecipherable problems, and unbearable situations. This condition causes anxiety and actual dread of coming to work each day.

Many people feel the situation is hopeless and believe they must just live with it. It is like a giant elephant in the living room. Everyone knows it is there and it just keeps tiptoeing around it—certainly not wanting to disturb it or cause further pain for themselves.

This "dramatic" model that I am presenting can bring new insights as well as help for people to learn personal responsibility. Managers and leaders can contribute significantly. They can create positive changes in their own environment when they themselves can become responsible for their own dramas.

The workplace actually provides infinite possibilities to awaken from the drama. As leaders, when you begin freeing yourself from the death grip of the ego, you will discover your authentic power—a power that is unlimited.

This framework of the theater can illustrate a way to create a new form of leadership, as well as a better way to relate in the workplace. As a leader, you will have the capacity to change the atmosphere at work to one of kindness and compassion.

As you address your own issues, you unhook from the ego drama, releasing others to do the same. You will become an enlightened leader who inspires people to higher levels of success and happiness. You will experience a deep satisfaction as you enrich the lives of others by freeing them to express their true beings.

As you do this, business will grow and prosper.

You are deeply ingrained in the way you operate in the world, so you will be tempted to return to old ways that the ego has of reacting to situations and people. However, the more you demonstrate to yourself and others the beauty of relating in the new way, the more the results will become perceptible and reinforcing.

Your new leadership style will bring you positive results with those you lead. You will experience a new kind of peace and satisfaction that has been missing or forgotten in your career and in your life.

At times, the ego will tempt you to return to its ways. Or you may be hooked into reacting to another's ego. That is why it is important to take steps to implement and practice the steps in this book on a continual and daily basis in order to strengthen your "enlightened" behavior.

This new way of leading and communicating will be well worth the effort. Your organization will thrive and grow as it never has before. You will create a team of people coming together with the synergism and power of a shared vision, which can never occur in the ego-drama world of individual plots and schemes.

Learning to recognize the spiritual essence in yourself and others is the key to enlightened leadership. It is the only path to long-term success for an organization.

As a leader, you will be the key to changing the drama, the plot, and the on-going scenes on the stage of the workplace. Doubt and fear will come along the way, but your commitment and dedication will be rewarded if you dare to look behind the face of the ego.

Who would choose the tiny, artificial power of the ego, even if for only a moment, once the authentic power of spirit has been recognized?

As you get a glimpse of how truly awesome you are, it will be hard to go back.

PART II

SHINING THE SPOTLIGHT
ON THE STAGE
AT WORK

CHAPTER FOUR

The Star (Protagonist) and Theme

Seeing the workplace as a stage, with a dramatic performance being played out, can help you see that it is just not real; it is an illusion. However, as long as you participate in the drama and play your parts, it will seem real.

The ego is dependent on the drama to ensure its identity because, without that external reinforcement, its powerlessness would be revealed.

By recognizing that we created the script and directed our starring role will be a huge advancement in our evolution of healing our pain. Ultimately, it will heal our souls.

Furthermore, identifying the behavior and then the companion emotions (that you keep replaying in the same scenes) will bring about a new understanding of yourself and your ego's role. It will allow you to escape the endless trap of pain and suffering that is based on a false belief system, constructed from the past. This will be of great usefulness because you will no longer be controlled by the ego of yourself or others.

You will begin to uncover your hidden motives, which direct the action in your drama. You will become powerful in your ability to change the script. You will be able to release your role as a helpless victim and take on a new role, your true role, coming from authentic power. And as you do that, you also will also be helping others to awaken from their drama as well.

This book is about a restoration process—the restoration of you to your soul, your highest self. If you have hidden agendas, designed by the ego, your progress will be limited.

Waking up requires strong focus and intent to reach your essence. This means bringing clarity to the drama in which you are participating. The model of a dramatic performance can help you see how this illusion is maintained, and it will help you begin to step out of the drama and step into reality.

Let us take a more detailed look at the performance that is occurring in almost every business in the country, and discover how you partake and define yourself in it.

You have created an identity and starring role in your version of the drama. The workplace is the current stage where most of the drama is taking place. Of course, some of the daily scenes get replayed at home with your family and you probably have starring roles on other stages in your life, such as social groups, political groups, etc.

But the primary stage, in terms of time, for most people, is the workplace. That is where you spend eight or more hours of each weekday, not including all the outside time spent working on or worrying about your job. It is a major stage. It is here that you gain your professional status, create a sense of identity in the world, provide for your family's financial security, and create an economic lifestyle.

This stage cannot be taken lightly.

THE STAR OR PROTAGONIST OF THE DRAMA

Since the ego is an actor created to cope and operate in a world of other actors, it would naturally have the starring role in the drama in which it acts.

The protagonist in a literary drama is the dynamic character who faces the challenges and conflicts of the story line. The story revolves around the star's actions, words, thoughts, and reactions as the star meets up and interacts with other characters who also help create the drama.

In order to understand the protagonist, we must know about its background, its appearance, its personality, its motivations, its relationships, its conflicts, and its changes as the character progresses through the dramatic episodes of the story.

There are many kinds of heroes in epic dramas and tragedies that we see in the theater. The journey of the hero is usually that of suffering and despair, leading to triumph and victory in some form. A tragedy, on the other hand, shows the downfall or destruction of a noble or outstanding person who has a tragic flaw or character weakness. The person is not all good nor all bad, so when reading or watching a tragedy, we usually feel mixed emotions. Sacrifice is usually a central theme in the experience of a tragic hero and often ends in death.

Playing out the role of the victim or martyr is a phase many heroes must pass through. Slaying dragons and discovering internal power finally leads to resolution of some kind in the happy ending dramas. A tragedy occurs when the hero is overcome, even after fighting valiantly.

There are many universal themes throughout history that are portrayed in the books we read and in the dramas we attend. What we don't realize is that our own real lives are cast and played out by unconsciously following one or more of these universal themes.

Discovering the source of inner strength and then changing the direction of your own starring role and script can be the way to enlightenment and self-transformation.

THE STAR AND ITS THEME

Let's take a look at the ego as the star of its drama and the originator of the theme that leads the ego through its workday and its life.

The star of your reoccurring drama follows the theme that depicts your character as a hero on a journey of trials and tribulations, challenges and conflicts. The ego believes you will ultimately find a happy and dramatic ending. This journey is unknowingly a plan to awaken you from this recreation of the past and a belief system that you developed long ago.

But the path of getting there is one of tragedy and pain, until you surrender the ego's performance in favor of the road back to your authentic self.

For centuries, universal themes have been the source of drama and the possibility for transformation. Individuals throughout history have followed these paths of self-discovery through a tragedy of conflict, sacrifice, pain, and suffering that ultimately leads to a resolution or a tragic ending.

Recognizing your theme and your starring role can be of great assistance to you in uncovering your inner motives and discovering your true self, if you choose to learn the lessons presented.

Some of the themes we see played out in books and movies are very familiar and common. We see tragedies in movies of long suffering, such as in *Terms of Endearment* and *Steel Magnolias*. The-shattered-illusion-and-destruction-of-the-hero theme shows up in *Death of a Salesman* and many of Shakespeare's tragedies, like *Hamlet*.

The Cinderella story is a reoccurring theme in such movies as *Pretty Woman* and *My Fair Lady*. Rags to riches stories are very popular, such as *Oliver* and *Annie*. *Joan of Arc*, *Ghandi*, and *Christ* depict the theme of great sacrifice for the good of humanity. *Rocky*, *The Karate Kid*, and many other books and movies depict the story of how the underdog, through perseverance and triumphs, becomes the victor. Star-crossed lovers are the central basis for dramas, such as *Romeo and Juliet* and *West Side Story*.

Hero/warrior stories are probably the most common with the hero fighting dragons and winning the kingdom. This theme is seen in war stories, westerns, cop shows, epic adventures, and science fiction, to name a few. *Indiana Jones* and *James Bond* are examples of the superhero who inspires our desire to rise above the mundane.

We settle for mediocrity and smallness of the ego in our lives, but go to the movies to dream of power and greatness.

Goodness and morality, surviving over evil and greed, is the theme of a timeless movie watched every year by millions of people for the past four decades in *It's a Wonderful Life*. We all cry as everyone comes to the support of Jimmy Stewart's character for his heroic commitment to honesty and humanity when challenged by the greediness of the town bully.

There are many other universal themes, such as martyrdom, good versus evil, man's search for meaning, fighting oppression, rebellion and defiance, the strength of the human spirit, moral choices, destiny versus free will, unrequited love, the love triangle, man's struggle to fulfill his duty, betrayal and loss, good boy versus bad boy, and numerous others.

We identify with the star and the struggle because we relate to the theme in our own real life.

The star of your drama is the ego. It finds the challenges and dramatic support that is needed to fulfill its role without conscious knowledge. It occurs like it is *happening to you*. But that is not the case.

You are actually attracting the experiences and characters to you. The experiences, as you interact with other characters, are determined and driven by your past scenes of similar encounters.

It is extremely helpful to identify your theme and starring role to help you see how you are carrying out your drama in the workplace. Be aware that you may actually have more than one theme: one major theme and many other minor themes.

One way to help you discover your starring role and theme is to recall movies or books to which you related or that inspired you. If that is difficult to recognize, think of movies that you have really enjoyed in the past. Which ones stand out? Do they have a theme that you connect with or a starring character by which you feel moved or challenged?

The important thing to understand is that the theme leads the character to the places in his soul that needs healing. Other characters in the story become a mirror to show the main character—you—the issues and struggles that you cannot see without interacting with others.

Much like a sound wave needing to impact an object to resonate sound, you need other characters to see yourself.

You, as the star, repeatedly play out your theme. It began in childhood and is carried throughout your adulthood, even though it has been disguised to you. It will continue to run your life until something happens to get your attention. This is usually a crisis or some great discomfort.

Recognizing your theme and role in the drama can be a shortcut to help you see how you unconsciously play out your scenes in the workplace. Recognizing your theme can give you the freedom of choice in how your story ends, rather than having it reach that critical stage. This can assist you in breaking out of the role, without having to crash and burn first.

Identifying your starring role and acknowledging your theme is the opportunity to get off the elevator on the upper floor, rather than having to wait until it hits rock bottom. It takes some deep probing and a willingness to give up some of the pride of the ego to make this discovery. Seeing some humor in the process can help.

A pediatrician, Dr. Michael Jones, discovered that his theme was that it was "noble to suffer." His father had abused him as a child, and he actually broke Michael's arm when he was five years old because he couldn't tie his shoes. He was also locked outside in the dark and suffered innumerable beatings. Michael's theme became his way of life.

But his theme also brought into his life more suffering. He had been mistreated and emotionally and/or economically abused by his wife, his stockbroker, his tenants, and others. His discovery that he was a frequent victim, due to his theme, caused a huge breakthrough.

He then took charge of his life and began taking a stand for himself. He no longer needed to suffer when he recognized it was just a belief system from his past that he kept replaying. His theme was not real.

Now he contributes to the world from a powerful position, not one of a suffering victim.

Some good came from his theme and starring role: that of helping children by being a caring and dedicated doctor.

George was a powerful businessman who unconsciously employed the dictator/bully method of leadership. He was demanding of his employees and very intimidating to everyone who dealt with him at work and elsewhere.

George discovered that his theme of being the dictator/ bully originated in his past, also. He had been very overweight as a child and was never good in sports. He was rarely chosen for any teams, and the girls seldom liked him. He began fighting back by being the smartest and the toughest in his class.

He told me about a time when he was a teen-ager and he had bought a used car. Suddenly he became popular with kids who wanted him to drive them to the beach. This became a weekly Saturday event. George secretly knew that he was being used, but so desperate was he for friends and socialization that he closed his eyes to the truth.

One weekend, another kid in the group offered to drive. They were all waiting on the corner to be picked up; but when the boy arrived, he was driving a very small car. It was obvious they wouldn't all fit in the car. George, being the largest, was the one who would take up the most room. They all looked at him with embarrassed expressions that clearly suggested he should be the one to drop out. He told the group he had to mow the lawn, anyway, and for them to go along without him.

Crushed by the rejection, that was the day that he decided no one was ever going to hurt or overpower him again. He unconsciously solidified his theme of power and strength through intimidation, believing that would protect him and keep him safe from rejection.

Recognizing his theme and his starring role was important because George discovered that his theme, although giving him an illusion of safety, was also preventing him from having love in his life.

As he gave up following his familiar theme, his business became even more prosperous with employees who were happier and more productive, and his personal life changed as well, to include new friends, activities, and a better marriage. The change in his life was dramatic.

The interesting thing about the starring role and theme is that the star does not usually recognize the way others perceive him or her.

George was quite surprised to discover that people didn't like him and were very fearful of him. He thought they respected him and their actions were a demonstration of their admiration. He was hurt and then transformed as he challenged his theme and his leading role to become a man of compassion, instead.

Michael, the doctor, did not realize he was attracting the experiences of abuse to himself because of his suffering victim identity. He thought this was happening to him because that is just the way life is.

When you recognize the ego's theme and see how you keep going down the same path, you can then begin to find out the true and worthwhile theme of the soul: that of discovering who you really are.

It is a tall order because you have been operating from the ego identity all your life, but as you begin realizing that this identity is not who you are, you will begin to see your true purpose and destiny.

If you want to know what your great lessons are, look at what hurts you, what you are afraid of, and when you are trying to be superior. What are you hiding?

Nourishing your inner spirit is essential to a fulfilling and purposeful life. Facing your ego and challenging the force of its tightly held grip on you will lead to a truly expansive experience. You will discover the majestic hero that you really are—a soul of great dimension and power, capable of going far beyond the tiny expectations and imagination of the ego.

You will see that the ego is afraid and uncertain. Your ego cowers in the face of your immortal and true self that resides beneath the drama in which you are starring.

IDENTIFYING YOUR THEME

Getting just a glimpse of yourself, in your persistent starring role and theme so that you see how you have been acting out this role, will start the process of unlocking the door to your inner greatness. The more you observe this repeated performance, the greater the opportunity for you to give it up. As you give it up, you can then embark on the true path—that of becoming whole and complete.

Your ego will resist this, however, because the ego does not want you to discover your authentic self . . . for that will be the end of the ego.

If you are unable to identify your starring role and theme, you can ask other people how they see you. Tell them you want them to be very candid and describe to you the character from a movie or book that they think is most similar to you. Ask them to describe characteristics that they observe in you.

Using a favorite movie/book or asking someone else for their viewpoint helps you see your possible theme and characterization of yourself from a perspective that is at a higher level or in the bigger picture. We have trouble seeing our wants, our fears, our needs, and roles because we are so deep in our own drama.

The theme and the starring role are inescapably interwoven. The theme defines the path of the star. However, uncovering the theme and leading role will also enable you to discover the underlying, unconscious motives and plots, which are the essential basis for the direction of the drama.

Recognizing these unconscious goals and needs for evidence in your drama will help you identify the automatic behavior and unvarying role in which you cast yourself. Finding your *modus operandi* can help unravel the mystery of your confusion and suffering.

The enemy that you believe is outside yourself is actually defined by you, based on similar scenes that occurred in the past.

Your role, as the star, is not the real. However, benign as it may appear, it does prevent you from grasping your full power, your natural inheritance, and your ability to be all that you choose. The drama keeps you reliving the ancient past that is not real and stops you from being in the present moment.

Remember that the past is only a memory, and recreating it is a pointless journey. It is over. You are in today and that is all you have.

Let's look at your life to discover your starring role and theme(s). Ask yourself some of the following questions:

- When I was growing up, what was I most praised for?
- What has been my greatest achievement?
- For what would I want to be remembered?
- What qualities would others use to describe me?
- What obstacles have I overcome?
- What have I had to endure?
- Who have been my adversaries? Why?
- What have been my biggest misfortunes?
- If I had to choose a character in a movie or book that most resembles me and my life theme, who would it be? (You may have more than one.)
- What is my greatest character strength?

As you answer those questions, a theme or pattern which reoccurs will probably emerge.

Your theme is one in which you feel comfortable and is familiar, even though it is the source of despair and anguish at times. Your leading star personality is one that you are proud of and fulfills your image of whom you believe you should be.

But your ego identity also has fears of inadequacy that it tries to mask, even from you.

Marsha was an account executive for a high tech company and was a great sales producer, exceeding her quotas most of the time. She was very attractive and always dressed in the latest fashions. She had a vibrant and vivacious personality that made her a guest on everyone's list. Men followed her around like flies, and she always had her choice of men to date. As one short-term relationship would end, another man would immediately appear from the wings. Her friends viewed her as confident, outgoing, and extremely able, both in work and social situations. Her girlfriends envied her capacity to find available men in a world where they were complaining, "There aren't any single men."

Marsha had no trouble recognizing her role and theme as that of Scarlet O'Hara in *Gone with the Wind*. She saw herself as the center of men's attention, but also being a passionate woman who had a strong will. She was proud of this image and enjoyed the success in her career.

However, Marsha shared with me her loneliness and actual desire to have a long-term committed relationship. In addition, unbeknownst to her company, she was actually nearing a "burnout stage" in her career. The constant pressure to produce, meet quotas, and work harder and harder was taking a toll on her.

When we probed deeper, it became apparent to Marsha that her role as Scarlet was, indeed, an Academy Award Performance because Marsha's real fear was that she wasn't attractive enough, good enough, or worthy of being the one someone chose for a permanent partner.

Her role as Scarlet was her ego's attempt to deny her inner fears by demonstrating to the world that she could take care of herself, be extremely successful, and have any man she wanted.

However, it was in her intimate relationships that the fear emerged. She unconsciously sabotaged the possibility of a love relationship by alternating between confidence and need. Not knowing her authentic power and the truth that she deserved to be loved, she was unable to be her real self in relationships and, ultimately, either he or she left.

Her theme was originated in childhood when she felt lost in the crowd of a large family of girls, where she never felt the love and attention she needed. So she developed the ego and personality to get what she needed.

This role served her well in the workplace as an overachiever with an outgoing, tenacious personality. However, she was tired of that competitive environment in the workplace and also wanted love in her life.

As Marsha gave up pretending and started the authentic path to her inner spirit, her life began to change. She dated fewer men but the quality of the relationships changed as she gave up her starring role. Her sales production remained high, but she reported having more peace and time for other pleasures in her life.

Playing the high performance role had taken a lot of energy that then became available for other activities. Her frenzied schedule and demands of the ego had exhausted her. She now discovered new vitality and energy by aligning with her spirit.

I am sure her life will continue to improve as long as she stays committed to fulfilling her soul's purpose, which includes having love and compassion for herself.

Richard was a vice president with a large bank and seemed to have the world at his fingertips. He had a beautiful wife, a successful career, and two children—the American dream.

While I was working with his bank, Richard and I discussed his starring role and theme. Richard saw himself as the triumphant hero who always achieved victory and high acclaim. His theme of winning and being the brightest and best seemed to be working for him, based on his level of corporate status in the bank.

However, talking with other members of the bank, it was revealed that Richard was a "know-it-all" who never allowed others to contribute. His arrogance was well-known throughout the branches. And it was not a secret that he had several affairs and that he was fortunate that he hadn't had sexual harassments suits filed against him.

He was seen not as the brilliant hero he believed himself to be, but, instead seen by co-workers and staff as a pompous man, lacking integrity. He was not a good leader; and his team, although they performed well, did so, in spite of him, and not because he helped them reach their potential.

It was a couple months later that Richard confessed to me that his wife was filing for a divorce. He was devastated.

We revisited his starring role and theme, and he discovered the denial his ego was holding in place to keep him from facing his immense fear.

When Richard was a boy, he had a very controlling mother who had very high expectations of him. She was very critical and demanding, and showed very little affection. Richard became the star of every team and had the best grades in every class. He was the valedictorian as well as a lettered athlete. It seemed there was nothing Richard couldn't do.

His belief that he was not lovable was made worse with the companion torment of not wanting to be exposed as the "wrong little boy." His starring role was a mask for a little boy who was desperately afraid.

Richard was not connected to his inner spirit or his authentic power. So all the accolades, and even the attention from women, would not fill the void in his psyche. Richard was finally ready to begin giving up his starring role and womanizer theme.

Richard's life began to change.

Unfortunately, it took great pain and anguish to look behind the face of his ego. But as he did, his leadership style improved, and people reported working in a better environment. His wife still filed for divorce; but, with time, perhaps their relationship will improve if he remains committed to awakening from his false drama.

WAKING UP FROM YOUR DRAMA

As you start recognizing your theme and leading role, you will see the workplace and your life differently. Initially, however, you will continue to play out your role. Little by little, you will begin to see the falsity of your play-acting. You will start "waking up" and seeing another way of responding to situations and people.

The desire to stay asleep in your drama is quite prevalent. The average person is living life on a day-to-day basis, unaware of being asleep. The individual assumes everyone else is living his or her life in the same manner with varying degrees of so-called success. Most people rarely question anything, but merely accept that this is one's lot in life.

However, in everyone's life, periodically, an opportunity for learning and for healing occurs. These chances for growth usually come disguised as obstacles or painful situations. Sometimes they are a loss of a job or a loved one; or other possible economic, emotional, or physical hardships. These challenging times can be the best learning opportunities . . . if the person so chooses.

Today, you have many chances to start unhooking from the painful web of so much suffering in the workplace, the constant interaction with other egos who hook your buttons, the high intensity of the overall work situation.

The important word here is *choice*.

There are four things that never change while living on this planet: time, choice, truth, and death.

During the allotment of time between birth and death, we have many passages and stages in which we can choose to see things differently. Having painful circumstances can be a blessing in disguise when it leads to new growth and evolution.

The interesting phenomenon about choice is that everyone has ample time to use that liberty. Freely choosing that which will advance the soul is the best course of action, but is usually not done because of the intense pressure from the ego to stay with the familiar theme.

If you do not choose spirit over ego, the lesson will continue to be presented. Your soul will actually direct you into further opportunities to wake up.

Unfortunately, the resulting pain with each new experience is usually intensified. This is because the early "wake-up calls" were ignored, and it takes more to get your attention.

So begin to identify, each day, how you follow a predetermined theme as you encounter people and events.

Watch your reactions and ask yourself the following questions:

- Is this helping reinforce my ego identity as the star of my drama?
- Am I discovering the center of my being, or am I simply gaining strokes for my ego and its drama?
- Do I really need to be the star?
- Am I expecting others to play a role in my drama?
- Am I listening to what others really say or do? Do I have a script for them?
- Am I meeting my ego needs at the expense of others?
- Am I blaming others for my suffering?

To assist yourself in awakening from this drama, start to challenge some of the automatic ways you have been spending your day. Change some of the daily routines that you do that have become so habitual. Let go of some of the structure, and allow more spontaneity in your life.

The ego keeps you numb. By awakening to your environment through your senses, you will become more present and aware of your life.

The following activities would be a good place to start:

- Take a different route to work.
- Buy clothes that are a different style or color than you usually select.
- Eat lunch at a new restaurant.
- Go to lunch with different people.
- Change meeting times and vary the agenda.
- Consciously look people in the eye.
- Walk instead of riding elevators, escalators, etc. whenever possible.
- Try a new food or recipe.
- Take a long bath and don't rush to get through it.
- Give yourself a treat—something frivolous. Examples: massage, ice cream cone, manicure, day off, extra round of golf, nap, anything new that you didn't think you should buy.
- Walk in the rain without an umbrella.

- Take a walk in a park.
- Say hello and smile at strangers.
- Wade in a lake or pond.
- Go to a good movie or theater without planning it ahead of time.
- Call someone you haven't talked to in a long time.
- Pay attention to colors, smells, textures, and sounds. Become more aware of your senses.
- Stop at least every hour when you are working and come out of intense concentration.
- Skip television and listen to music or read a book.
- Spend some quiet relaxation time when you first wake up and right before you go to bed.

These methods will aid in "waking you up," just as smelling coffee and bacon can awaken you in the morning. These variations in your routines assist you in being in the "now," which is all we have.

When we walk around numb or not "present" to our lives, it is indeed a tragedy.

Living on the surface and feeling vaguely satisfied are ways many people live. Waking up for people who are vaguely satisfied is more difficult than for those who are recognizing their pain, ready to seek another way. The semi-alive people will not see the need as greatly because they are in a state of resignation.

"This is as good as it gets" or "It could be worse" is their belief system. The fear of the unknown is greater than their discomfort, so it is easier to just go on as they are.

They will often describe themselves as happy the way they are. The truth is that they have not allowed themselves to feel their own pain. You know many people like this.

They could just continue on in this unsatisfying way, but life usually brings about situations that make it increasingly difficult to ignore their lack of true awareness and movement toward their true purpose.

Breaking through this consciousness of denial and automatic behavior is a process that occurs only when the person is ready and willing. Getting to that point often comes when there is pain, when there is enough pain to finally get your attention.

If the ego keeps the denial and substitutes in place (such as momentary pleasures, outside distractions, and external validation), the need to awaken from the drama is not felt so intensely. Even the misery in the workplace is denied as the ego uses all kinds of techniques to keep the pain below the surface to avoid acknowledging the ego's fears.

How long do you want to live your life in semi-happiness?

People are finally realizing this life is too precious to waste with the distress and sadness that are being perpetuated on the stage called the workplace.

Behind the ego is powerlessness.

When you confront your ego's fears, you will discover peace where you anticipated pain. You will start to see the ego is an actor with no authority. Seeking your starring role and finding out how your theme is controlling your life will bring new freedom.

When do we choose to learn the lessons presented in the workplace? When do we step off the stage and become the director of our life instead of an actor in a tragedy?

Why not now?

And as you do, it touches all those with whom you come in contact. You can be the light to help shine away the pain in this dimly lit drama.

CHAPTER FIVE

Motive and Plot

This book is an opportunity to shine light on the entanglement of egos in the workplace, so that the drama can be revealed and individuals can stop being hooked by their egos. This web of reacting egos is the source of the ever-escalating experience of envy and pain, victory and loss, and all other emotional interactions occurring on your workplace stage.

If we can believe that this world is only a reflection of reality and that we are playing out our evolution on a journey to a greater reality, then we can make efforts to awaken from this illusion. If we understand that purpose and potential are found in every interaction to help heal us and lead us to our inner selves, then we will find peace.

As we do this as individuals, we can bring an environment of peace to the workplace. As managers and leaders begin to understand the source of the fear and conflicts in the workplace, the consciousness will change. Companies will rise to new levels of success, achievement, and satisfaction when they transform the emotional dynamics.

PERSONAL RESPONSIBILITY

The problem today is that most people are assigning responsibility for their lives and life situations outside of themselves. This, of course, is coming from the viewpoint of the ego that feels powerless. All occurrences and situations are actually drawn to you, based on your own unconscious motives. There are no accidents.

It is as though there is a joint agreement of unseen but compelling cosmic forces.

This vortex of energy, made of intersecting beliefs, produces a magnetic power drawing the necessary players onto the workplace stage. Your beliefs and thoughts create a force that brings about situations and people that will interconnect with you. Together, you play out your drama of unconscious needs, desires, and motives.

In a sense, you use others to meet the needs of your play. Your thoughts and words have a will that manifests into reality.

When you complain about your life, you are actually giving up your own autonomy. The point of view that sees things as "happening to you" allows you to abdicate responsibility for your life. It accordingly relinquishes your power to do anything about it. This viewpoint and belief makes you a helpless victim.

Statements that deny your power always create undesirable results, and cause confusion and pain. Denying your power is your ego's decision. But your inner spirit is totally aware of your unlimited power.

This way of viewing the world as a victim is hard to reconcile. If you say, "It is not my fault; I am not to blame for the things that have gone wrong in my life," your ego feels relieved. Your ego wants to be right and does not want to claim any accountability for that which has *not turned out the way you want.* So the ego gets to maintain its innocence.

But when events or circumstances *do turn out the way you want,* your ego wants to declare ownership and victory.

So when are you to blame and when are you not? To clarify this, we need to better understand cause and effect.

Cause and effect are actually not opposites; they are really two parts of the same occurrence. There can be no effect without a cause; but conversely, there can be no cause without an effect. They are participating mutually in the same dynamic.

Most of us have this confused, so we immediately jump to finding fault in any incident and usually fully project the blame onto anyone, anyone but ourselves.

Being willing to see your participation in any cause-and-effect dynamic will free you from needing to deny or suppress motivations or fears. The very acknowledgment that you are neither a victim or a villain is both releasing and empowering.

To illustrate this relationship between cause and effect, picture a batter at home plate. There could be no hit or home run, no matter how many times the batter swings without the ball being in the air precisely at the moment the bat is swung. The pitcher could have thrown that ball perfectly across the plate; but without a batter swinging the bat, there would be no hit. The impact would not have occurred without this mutual cooperation.

So ultimately, cause and effect are one dynamic synchronistically occurring and being played out. There are, therefore, really no accidents.

But the ego has selective interpretations.

It will claim to be the "cause" or responsible for the result if you deem it a favorable outcome. The ego believes a worthy conclusion elevates your status in the world. Conversely, the ego will deny being the cause or being responsible for that which it feels is negative about you.

A good illustration of this is Craig, a divorced man with two children. He harbors a great sense of guilt for having divorced his wife when his children were young. He also feels remorse for not participating as a father in the early years of their childhood, due to his business distractions and other involvements outside the family.

When the children were young, he was not always emotionally available for them. The son is now in college and doing well. The younger daughter has not done so well. She has had all kinds of trouble, been involved in illegal drugs and done poorly in school. She rebels against the mother and is unreliable.

Craig's ego takes credit for the college-aged son's success, proving that he was a good father. However, he blames all the problems the daughter is having on the former wife, citing her lack of discipline and poor parenting skills as the cause. His ego believes this exonerates him from the responsibility of any cause-and-effect dynamics with the younger child.

Here we can see clearly the dichotomy: Craig is claiming the good outcome and denying the bad outcome.

However, this denial causes Craig more pain and energy because it is difficult to keep the fears and doubts about himself from surfacing. It also requires him to keep blaming the ex-wife and daughter for their failures. This prevents him from having any kind of relationship with his former wife or his daughter.

He loves his daughter, but his constant criticism of her and casting her as a failure have caused the daughter to alienate herself. Now Craig further complicates this situation by blaming the daughter for not wanting to see him or have a relationship with him. Now he has cast *himself* as the victim; the good father who is rejected.

Failing to see and admit to himself, that his daughter is acting out from pain in her psyche that occurred when the girl was very young, prevents Craig from having any compassion for his daughter and her unfortunate dilemma of chemical addiction. His critical and unsupportive approach to her continues to add to the girl's lack of self-worth.

Craig's ego continually gives his daughter the message that the she is a disappointment in his eyes. Then Craig wonders why his daughter does not want to see him. He does not recognize that his judgment is driving his daughter farther away and deeper into her addiction to alleviate the pain.

If this is hard to grasp, consider the powerlessness that comes from denying responsibility for consequences. Understand that all encounters in which you participate with another are actually mutual cause-and-effect dynamics.

Authentic power is willing to be the cause in any matter, whether the outcome is perceived as "good" or "bad."

Even willingness to give up being a victim and recognizing your willing participation in the "self-described" victim role will empower you. In reality, you are not powerless—only your self-created ego is weak. And that is the ultimate goal of this book:

to help you see that the ego is really powerless. As you do, you can begin to give up the drama, the blame, the self-validation, and the role of the victim.

Claiming your authentic inner power is the beginning of waking up and finding freedom.

What you so strongly want to deny, that which you feel you must defend, is the very thing you need to look at. The very acknowledgment and surrender, to what you fear or to what occurred, will release you from your self-made prison.

Craig's acknowledgment of his participation in the creation of his daughter's early environment would allow him to have compassion for her and her dysfunction. Craig would then be in a position of non-judgment and caring, which would allow the daughter the freedom to return to her father.

Accepting his responsibility and having empathy for his daughter would give Craig the opportunity to truly help his daughter. However, as long as he is in denial of his responsibility, this will not occur.

So being responsible is really just claiming the power that you already have, but have been denying.

When you truly see how powerful you are, you can consciously use your genuine power for the creation of peace, joy, and love in your life and the lives of others around you. You will stop creating the dramas that come from believing you are helpless and, instead, create a new world where trust and compassion prevail.

DISCOVERING YOUR UNCONSCIOUS MOTIVES AND PLOT

Every drama has a plot. As the star of your performance, you are following a story line that will seek evidence to prove your motives.

The plot in your drama does not change because you created it from unconscious motives and continue to play it out with the same goals. Although the players may change, the drama will not vary because you originated the plot to recreate and prove your belief system developed in the past.

You may consciously think you are the victim of the drama and that the other players are to blame, but that is not the case.

You may believe you are seeking a new outcome, and you may genuinely feel that you are trying to bring about a change in your life. But unless you change the motives and reassign the roles in your drama, nothing will change.

You will continue the same performance with possible changes in the cast of characters. Or you may move to a different stage or workplace. But the scenes will be the same with a similar ending to the story.

Your ego actually needs the people in the workplace to interact with you to validate your story. The other players, who take significant roles in your play, reinforce and support your plot. And in the end, you get to be right, once again!

Your ego's goal is to always find evidence to support your story line and your belief that it is not your fault. The other characters have the same goal, coming from different unconscious motives and plots.

As the emotional intensity increases in the workplace, which it always does, you must play out your part with mounting passion. As your emotional fervor builds, the other egos in the workplace react with rising vehemence. The plot thickens as the drama escalates.

The resulting scenes cause ever-increasing complexity and make it almost impossible to recognize the origin or even the point. The momentum of these racking emotions take over, and the result becomes literally a scene from "As the Stomach Turns."

The ego's plan is forever the same and will always lead to the same consequences your plot demands, even if it is painful or disappointing on a conscious level. You unconsciously will find what substantiates your belief system from the past, and that will satisfy your need to be blameless.

So why don't you just change it? It is actually that simple: change your mind, and the motives and drama will change.

However, the ego wants the drama to continue. So while you are operating from the ego, you cannot see that you originated it. It feels out of your control and appears to be happening to you.

What does it take to change your mind?

It begins with challenging yourself to discover the unconscious motives that direct your plot. A place to start is to begin noticing when your ego gets hooked and then gently ask yourself the following:

- What am I defending or trying to hide?
- What do I think the reaction of others says about me?
- What am I afraid of?
- What do I think will happen?
- When did I feel this way before?

Only by interacting with others and discovering your fears can you dislodge the hidden doubts and pains, which are the source of your motives and ultimate drama.

Learn to observe yourself and notice your language. What are you trying to keep below the surface? Any statement from you has authority and command.

When the outcome from our statement is desirable, we claim it. If something we consider negative or bad is occurring, we say it is happening to us. But even negative phraseology comes to fruition because you create your world with your thoughts and words.

Look behind your denials and negative statements. Look for the fear that they are hiding.

A small example is the statement, "I am not nervous." The very sentence creates the image of being nervous and will actually result in nervousness.

"I don't need anybody" is covering the fear that you do need somebody. If you truly don't need anyone, it wouldn't occur to you to say it. "I am calm" and "I am whole and complete" give you powerful results and freedom to choose what you want.

Your unconscious motives need to be revealed, by looking behind the face of the ego, to discover what you so valiantly defend. You need to expose your plot and motives to the light of day.

The drama and plot will never be different, as long as the motives remain unconscious and hidden from you. Your ego makes presumptions, based on the past, and sees the plot unfolding according to its script from past scenes.

Purposeful intention with right action can bring about a change in circumstances. This takes courage because the ego is so demanding and unforgiving. It holds others responsible and will not let go of its tenacious grip on you without a great deal of resistance.

You will be tempted to deny that pain is below the surface because, when you allow it to emerge, you will then have to deal with it. That is bad news for your ego, but good news for your soul.

William was a senior vice president in a large hospital. He had been with the hospital for years, and had always been a dedicated and committed individual. He was somewhat on the serious side and very analytical in his approach to management. Every person in his management group had very clear and specific performance objectives. He was relentless in assuring they were carried out—a good example of the micromanager. He exerted intense control over all those he managed and nothing slipped by him.

When the hospital hired a new CEO, William was somewhat nervous about the change in authority. The previous CEO had been in command for nearly thirty years and this new change made William uneasy. He didn't know what to expect with the new management in place. William performed best when everything was in his control.

The new CEO seemed very dynamic and confident, but he made William suspicious.

It became fairly clear rather rapidly that the new CEO would be making some sweeping changes. As the weeks progressed, William felt insecure in his formerly well-grounded position with the hospital.

As this uneasiness within himself increased, he began exerting more pressure and control on his staff. The employees, who were already unhappy under William's style, began to feel even more anxiety and stress from the increased watchfulness and strict demands made by him.

Within a few months, when the CEO had finished ascertaining the various roles and performances of different departments, William was offered an early retirement, which left him little choice. The control, that he had tried to enforce in an effort to make himself look good and keep himself safe, backfired.

William was devastated and forced to step off the stage, where he had spent most of his adult life. He spent almost a year blaming the new CEO and claiming his role as a righteous victim.

Because he was too young to want to retire from the workplace, William found another job. This time, because of the previous pain, he began to observe himself in a management position. William began to uncover the origin of his need for this over-diligent control of others and situations.

He had grown up an only child with very few playmates. His parents were overprotective and did little to encourage him to take risks or try new things. He was always a good student but very timid. He learned to operate in a small world with very little exploration because it felt safe and secure. The last thing he wanted was to call attention to himself in any way.

Because of his education, dedication, and faithfulness, he was finally promoted to a vice president at the hospital. His management style was never questioned and only the people who worked in his department knew what an unhappy environment it was.

William's unconscious motive was to keep everything and everyone in place. His fearful ego led him to believe that this would keep him protected.

It finally proved to be wrong.

As William began to open up with the new people and trust that they were capable of performing without a whip and checklist, he began feeling a new sense of freedom. He hadn't realized that enforcing all the rules in his former over-diligent manner was actually exhausting him.

He has continued to challenge his fears and give up the high control in his life, both at work and home. He is now happier in this new role on a new stage—only because he finally looked behind the face of his ego and at its unconscious motives—but it took a great disappointment and much pain to get his attention.

When we follow our unconscious motives, we are actually following the motives of the ego. Our goal is to bring them to light, release them, and create conscious goals and intentions that lead us to peace and understanding.

The work on yourself is difficult. You have to flush out the impurities and remove the blocks that you are defending and trying to keep in place. But the work is rewarding as you claim your rightful heritage, your true source, and your unlimited power and abilities.

EGO-DEFENSE MECHANISMS

The proof that the ego's thought system is so strong is demonstrated by the intense desire the ego has of denying any fears of doubts lying below the surface. The defensive posture is used to protect yourself from looking in the mirror that reflects the very issues you need to address to heal your soul. It is a mirror that the ego would prefer not to look into.

The ego responds to a perceived threat with an instinctive fight-or-flight pattern. Wanting to leave an uncomfortable circumstance rather than look behind the fear, the ego will instruct you to bail out or put on the boxing gloves. The decision is usually decided in a flash because your ego will react immediately, rather than allowing the communication to enter unhampered.

If you leave the situation, you will only encounter it again under similar circumstances. Unless you change your underlying motives, your story will continue to have the same scenes. Leaving one stage for another may give temporary relief from anxiety, but it is only a short-term response to stress and threats.

If you do not leave but choose to remain in the confrontation, your ego will direct a strategy to barricade and protect you. This ego–defense mechanism actually becomes an offense because the intention is to overcome or injure the source of the threat so that you will remain unscathed.

On the stage of human dynamics, there are no actions that do not result in consequences. Denial is a tool, used by your ego, to prevent you from looking within. Attacking another merely escalates the drama and keeps your energy involved with the drama.

If you find yourself defending anything, you can be certain that the very need to defend is an indication that something deeper is going on within you. When the perceived attack has no meaning, your ego is not called forth to protect you.

For example, if you are an excellent accountant and someone challenges your math, you would simply take a look at the financials and admit the error as a simple mistake. You would probably just correct it and reprint a new report. However, if you were concerned that your accounting abilities were weak and your job was dependent on your skills, your ego would react quickly to defend your mistake, believing it would be costly to your security to have been less than proficient.

I have heard people in the workplace say that they are sometimes required to defend their position or prove that their plan is a good one. I have also heard people say that they have had to stand up and defend their honor.

Your honor or your position does not need defending. Defending anything takes a great deal of energy and attention. It requires covering yourself from having any weaknesses exposed. What a shame. What a tragedy to be unable to acknowledge and receive support in areas where you don't have all the answers.

But the ego believes it must have all the answers and solutions, or it says something negative about you. And if you already have everything you need, why would you need anyone else? Why have a team? Why come together with others at all?

Defense is the main strategy of the ego because if you were to look at what it is you are defending, it would be the end of the ego.

You would discover that where you anticipated pain, you find peace and joy. You would learn that your inner spirit is capable of unlimited accomplishments and can be counted on in all situations. You would find a new kind of serenity, based not on being superior or overcoming others, but based simply on relying on your own authentic power of love and compassion.

The intensity of your defensive reaction can be a place for you to discover an opening to your inner self.

If you feel a great deal of emotion around a particular issue, it is because it is one of your bigger life lessons trying to present itself to you. The ego will naturally block this opportunity because your ego cowers in the face of your inner, true power.

The ego would rather have you rely on its tiny acting role as star of your drama. No matter how stellar the performance, it pales in comparison to your mighty, eternal, unalterable inner source.

One reason that we avoid looking within, to discover our issues, is that there is guilt and humiliation associated with hidden fears. There is a concealed core belief, beneath the surface, that is self-defacing and shameful.

The ego cannot accept any perception of weakness, believing that to be its Achilles' heel. Unbeknown to you, shining light on the origin of this belief is the key to freedom.

Getting past the ego's defenses is not easy. It stands as a guard at the door of your psyche, allowing only beliefs that support its fear to enter.

Let's look at Sheila's story and her unconscious motives to help us illuminate how underlying motives directed her plot and story line, even as it led to a descent into the depths of pain and suffering.

As the director of operations for a company that is highly successful, Sheila often felt put upon to carry the burden of the organization's structure and daily operations. Believing that no one was as knowledgeable as she (and certainly not as dedicated), she worked long and tedious hours. Her family complained that she was never home on time, and she herself begrudged the fact that she had little freedom for family and leisure.

Sheila's children had been disappointed numerous times when she did not arrive to watch them perform in school functions. Her husband often had to take up the slack, even though his position with his company was just as important and critical to his company's success. Yet, he somehow managed to work regular hours and have time for the family.

As the years passed by, her promise to her family that "things would get better" just never materialized. Her endless commitment to work continued.

It was not until her children started having serious problems that she began to question her obligation to her company. She felt incredible guilt when the counselor described the children as having a lack of her parental support and love during their critical years.

Although her husband had done as much as he could, the children had often felt abandoned by their mother. Their sense of self-esteem had suffered. Sheila's husband was on the verge of filing for divorce because the stress and lack of communication had mounted to unbearable levels.

Through counseling, Sheila began to look at what was driving her to such levels of workaholism. In actuality, the hours she was keeping at her company were not really required if she would have worked more efficiently and delegated some of the work to her staff.

The unconscious motives that surfaced for Sheila were a result of her early childhood fears of abandonment by her parents.

Sheila was the oldest in a family of five children. Her parents were often gone and did little to attend to the children. She was unconsciously angry at her father's lack of discipline and depressed by her mother's frequent absence. She began taking over many of the responsibilities of the mother: ironing, cleaning, cooking, and watching the younger children. It was an effort to please her parents and hold everything together.

Her efforts were not rewarded, so she felt victim of an unfair world.

When her friends were having fun going to parties and school dances, she was often bearing the responsibility of her siblings and the household. She hated her life, but Sheila felt she had no choice. She believed she was the only one responsible and accountable.

When she married her husband and had children, she always believed she would be a wonderful parent, having been for all intents and purposes, the "mother" for her sisters and brothers. However, her husband seemed to do such a good job with them and her job was so demanding that the years just slipped by.

Sheila finally recognized that the over-extended hours to her business were actually motivated by an unconscious desire to be the unappreciated, righteous martyr.

She saw that she somehow got a strange reinforcement when no one thanked her or gave her the praise she deserved. She finally saw that the lack of gratitude, offered by the company, gave her the "evidence" she sought, proving to herself that the world was still unfair and that she was the noble, sacrificing heroine of her drama.

The sad part of Sheila's story was the discovery that she had abandoned her own children, much as she had been abandoned as a child. But because she was able to acknowledge this unconscious action, she was able to stop defending her position.

Her ego's fear of being "wrong" and vulnerable diminished, and she started talking to her children from her authentic self.

She was able to establish a new relationship, based on honest communication, listening, and demonstrating compassion for them. She was able to ask them to forgive her for her continual focus on her job at their expense. Her relationship with her husband also changed as she gave up her martyr role.

When you uncover your unconscious motives, you can begin to start making conscious decisions and purposeful intentions.

Since all our motives (conscious and unconscious) have power to create, reclaiming your responsibility and your ability to set your intentions from your powerful source will change the direction of your drama.

CREATING CONSCIOUS MOTIVES

How do you recognize your unconscious motives before you hit the wall and have no choice but to seek a better way?

One way is to look at your life right now. Are you living the life you want? Are you at peace? Do you have the elements in your life story that fulfill your conscious wants and needs?

The life you are living, the family, the job, the home, the friends, and the lifestyle—all are results of your motives, whether they have been conscious or not.

There are no idle thoughts. We create our reality, based on our belief system, motives, and choices, whether realized or not.

If your life is not in harmony, you can know that you have contradictory goals. Your discordance is a result of conflicting desires and choices.

Begin looking at the areas in your life that are causing the discontentment. As you identify these undesirable areas, start to discern the possible rewards or reinforcement that you are receiving, in spite of your complaints about them.

Your true destiny is one of peace and contentment, joy and creativity, love and compassion. If you are not experiencing these feelings, then you are playing out a drama, based on contrary goals.

For example, Joan was a manager with much responsibility over several departments. She complained to me that the women in her workplace didn't like her and never included her in their conversations. However, it wasn't just her employees in her management groups, but other managers as well, who were cool to her.

I asked her if this had ever been a problem before. She conceded that there have been other situations when women didn't seem to care for her. She admitted that she thought they were probably jealous of her. She didn't understand why because she tried to be friendly.

"Why do you think they are jealous of you?" I asked.

She thought it was because she always dressed so professionally, was very efficient in her work, and had a few other positive qualities.

The interesting dilemma, I told her, was that I knew many women who dressed professionally, did an excellent job, etc. but *were liked* by their fellow female associates.

I asked her to gently try to look at herself as the possible source of the problem, instead of projecting it fully on the other female associates.

Joan had grown up in a family of very pretty sisters who were still very close. Joan had always felt she was the least attractive. In fact, she called herself the "ugly duckling." She had grown into a very attractive woman; but as a child, she had felt homely.

When she felt depressed as a child, she would go off to be by herself. The retreat from others gave her some relief and temporary peace.

Even as an adult, she was still striving to get her sisters' approval and continued to feel that she was not worthy of their attention. She still felt unequal to them in beauty and talent. This was a childhood belief system that was not true, but she lived her life as if it were factual.

She now began to realize that she sustained this theme of unworthiness into adulthood. She then found evidence to support her unconscious motive that women didn't like her. Her ego wanted to be right and wanted to believe that it wasn't her fault.

She started looking at ways she isolated herself at work that caused other women to distance themselves from her. She began noticing the things she did that would cause someone else to feel uncomfortable around her. She became aware that she often attempted to act superior among women in an effort to deny her actual feelings of being inferior.

Joan is now learning to recognize her unconscious motives. She is also beginning to make a *conscious intention* to extend herself to females at work, to work better with others, and even to have some fun at work.

If we looked at Joan's unconscious motives, we see that the ego is very deceptive. Joan had felt helpless to change the situation and was really very miserable and lonely in the workplace. Her ego, however, got the satisfaction of being right—the world is a cruel place, made up of cold-hearted and jealous women.

The key to the ego's unconscious motive is that it will always have a negative side, even as it seems to prove you are right in your viewpoint. And there will always be a loss or cost when your ego claims that you are the victim and that you are correct in your opinion.

For Joan, the cost was isolation and having no friends.

Do you want to discover your ego's unconscious motives? Do you want to begin releasing these motives that lead to your unvarying plot to gain proof? If you do, it takes willingness to be the cause of your life, to stop being the victim, and to courageously face your ego's fears.

The following questions will help you take the steps to do this:

- What makes you most unhappy in your life?
- Who is your ego blaming for these consequences?

- Do you notice any defenses or denials? Ask yourself, "What am I defending?"
- Although a situation makes you unhappy, what about it do you get to claim that makes it right?
- Do you say to yourself, "Perhaps I am wrong; perhaps there is another way to see this"? Can you find another way?
- When in the past did you feel a similar way in a similar situation?
- What is the cost or loss in your life when you maintain your ego's position of being right?
- What would be a new conscious intention to replace the ego's unconscious motive?

Let me warn you that this may take a lot of practice. The ego does not give up being right very easily.

Your ego will want to resist looking at itself as the source of pain. It will look most easily at others for blame and then find evidence to support that belief. It is hardest to stop this process of blaming when you are in the middle of a heated situation.

Here's an example of something I did in the middle of an argument with someone I cared very much about.

We had come to a toe-to-toe confrontation of two egos, each of us wanting to be right. We were at the point of hanging up on each other, of giving up trying to find resolution, when I said: "This is a perfect example of two egos battling—each wanting to be right. One of us needs to stop and look behind the face of our ego and to stop trying to win."

"I don't know how to do that," he told me.

I didn't know if I could do it either, so strong were the emotions going back and forth between us.

I decided to try.

Although I was feeling very angry, I stopped myself in the moment and said, "I'm sorry I'm being so insistent that I'm right. It really isn't my intention to hurt you or make you miserable"—which was exactly what he was feeling, as was I.

I was trying to look at what this lesson was telling me about myself and also trying to see his point of view.

"I want to hear what you're trying to say. It's my intention to understand you."

As I said these words, I began to feel myself calm down. As I continued, soon I started to feel sincere in my words.

The pain and anger I was feeling only a few moments ago began to dissipate as I gave up my unconscious motive to be right and to win. I realized we were each feeling like a victim, even though neither of us really was.

I changed my motive to a conscious intention of finding peace and resolution between us. I gave up my ego pride and the need to prevail. And we both benefited.

The wonderful thing, about giving up needing to be right and choosing to learn the lesson presented, is that it releases the other person from needing to maintain his position. The other person usually learns the lesson almost simultaneously because he can then stop feeling the need to blame you.

In my case, my friend immediately said that he also wanted to understand his lesson and that he also cared about my feelings. We were able to move forward in our relationship. We had learned it was possible to give up the battle, even in a heated moment. We were both then truly the winners.

Practicing these opportunities to become free of the ego and the unconscious motives takes perseverance and the belief that you are worth it. I have found it helps to go to a quiet place.

There, you can invoke your inner spirit to help you get past the formidable gates of your ego. Your ego takes it as a personal affront to point the finger at yourself. But that is the beginning of freedom, every time you do it.

If you are having a really difficult time looking at yourself as the source, you need to ask your inner spirit for the courage and guidance to do this. Just before I go to bed at night has often been a good time for me to ask for clarity.

You may then have a dream or you might, upon awakening, suddenly have a clear picture or understanding of your role in your own suffering. Understanding that you have a powerful will, whether it is coming from the ego or the higher self, is important here.

So the intent of this chapter is to help you uncover hidden motives that are directing your life. By doing this, you will move toward integration of your self to your authentic self.

Becoming whole and complete, without the need of external validation and drama, is the destiny of every soul. Having conflicting beliefs and opposing motives is the source of our confusion and misery, in the workplace or any place else in our lives.

You willingly participate in all experiences and interactions. This actually means that you *will* yourself into the circumstances and relationships in your life. They didn't just happen while you were looking the other way.

But the past is over, and replaying those scenes is tiresome and painful. When you discover your belief system and motives that were concocted in your past, you are ready to make conscious intentions for the present.

Choose a new conscious, happier future by reclaiming your heritage for peace and satisfaction. Looking at the way your ego is hooked into the workplace can lead to some of the greatest opportunities for the evolution of your soul. Making new conscious intentions will dramatically alter your life both at work and at home.

CHAPTER SIX

The Director and Script

THE DIRECTOR

Let's look at how the ego works as the director and creator of the script for your starring role in the drama on the workplace stage.

The director can be recognized as a voice that is calling forth the direction, the action, and the outcome of the scenes. The direction is based on the ego's need for corroboration of its leading role of passion and, usually, suffering.

The voice of your ego is on non-stop auto-play and is so incessant that you are never without it. Even as you try to stop it, it will continue directing you. You listen to it and sometimes you will even argue with it, but it is never silent. The fact that it is not really you, but the voice of the ego, is demonstrated by the fact that you can observe it and distinguish it from yourself when you focus and become present.

The voice of the director takes on many different tones. Sometimes it is the sound of your mother, warning of impending danger. Sometimes it sounds panicky and other times, persuasive. Often it can sound like a critical voice, limiting your faith in yourself with statements such as: "You are not capable of doing that!" "You will fail and make a fool of yourself."

The inner saboteur's director voice is coming from your ego, which does not believe you can achieve your desires without the many external validations such as money, other people's approval, status, or some tangible support. This is because the director, coming from the voice of the ego, is attempting to hide its shameful secret that it is not worthy on its own.

The director believes you need other people to validate you, but the ego is also afraid and intimidated by others. This causes a peculiar kind of dilemma because you need that which you fear. It is like being drawn to a fire but also being afraid you will be burned.

The director will guide you through episode after episode and scene after scene to substantiate the ego's performance and protect you from harm or shame. Fearing others' criticism and needing others' support for the drama are the motivation behind the director's supervision.

Hearing the tone and origin of the director's voice can be very helpful in discovering that the director is just another aspect of the ego, coming from your past conditioning. Learning to become aware of that voice and identifying it, from the long-ago cast of characters in your life, can assist you in finding freedom and peace.

Sandra was a co-owner of a service business that was very successful. Her clients were other businesses and Sandra had developed a skillful presentation and had faith in her employee's abilities to carry out and deliver the service. Her partner was a man whom she had known for many years and they had formed the joint partnership about five years previously.

There were several other similar businesses in her area, and although her company was doing well, there were two other larger firms that were doing a bigger volume and had some of the key prestigious business clients. Frequently, Sandra was up against these competitors in a proposal process; and for some reason, even though her firm had demonstrated great success with some of their existing clients, she did not win very many engagements when she was up against one of the bigger firms.

Sandra was also having some problems with her partner. Even though they were equal partners and he was always polite to her, she felt he treated her in a subservient manner. When she tried to discuss this with him, he denied it. He basically dismissed it, and the conversation always ended with her feelings not heard.

When the company had their staff meetings, Sandra, again felt inferior in power, even though she was the co-owner. Her partner often took the lead in the meetings and then supported other people rather than Sandra on some major decisions.

In addition, Sandra had some problems with a couple of employees. Not by coincidence, these two were the same ones that her partner always seemed to agree with. This only compounded the problem. Although she had equal economic power, she acquiesced to him in running the business, even against her better judgment.

When I talked with Sandra, we began exploring why she was afraid to be more assertive with her partner. She said she knew there was something going on because, as miserable as she felt sometimes, she couldn't seem to stop herself from backing down and giving in to his wishes.

She also noted that, when they were giving a presentation to a prospective company, she felt less confident if he was with her. When she took other employees for the group presentations, she always performed much better and the employees often complimented her on her great skills.

So what was going on? Why was she feeling intimidated by her partner?

One thing she recognized that her partner failed to see, was that this dissension between them, as well as between her and the employees with whom he sided, was actually draining the positive energy force and potential from their business success in many ways. Their combined leadership was muddled at best, and that resulted in the employees resorting to gossip and alliances.

In Sandra's viewpoint, it was her partner's entire fault. The two employees were very opinionated and disloyal to her. She was angry inside but felt powerless to change it. So she just went home at night and complained to her husband. Nothing changed, except her stress level—it was increasing.

She met me one day after she had just learned she didn't get an account that she had worked very hard to land. We were in a restaurant, and as she started to tell me about it, she broke down and cried. Sandra was reaching her limit of pain and insecurity. I asked her what she was feeling about herself that was making her feel so inadequate. It was only one account. There would be others.

She couldn't explain it, but she felt like she was never good enough. As she talked, her comments about herself were very negative and self-defacing. At that point, she seemed totally lacking in confidence and inner spirit. Finally, she agreed to spend some quiet time by herself, and listen to herself to discover where those negative messages were coming from.

We met the next day. Sandra had finally realized that the voice she was hearing in her head was actually her dad's voice. He had been dead for twenty years!

The director of her drama was still the voice of her father, who was extremely demanding and always told both her and her sister that they just "didn't do anything quite well enough." He was punitive and insensitive and no matter how hard she tried, she could never please him.

Even when she did her very best, he always told her she could have done better. She now carried out a drama, based on the father's voice. Her motive was finding evidence that she would never be quite good enough, that she would always be second best.

It was a long held unconscious belief that she replayed over and over. The amazing (or not so amazing) part was that her partner had a similar commanding personality and her ego now responded to him just as she had reacted to her dad. She had actually replaced her dad with the partner to validate her belief that she was not good enough. So her partner hooked old beliefs, and by being a mirror to her deeply imbedded fears, she saw and was able to recognize them.

This brought incredible freedom to Sandra when she realized her feelings and emotions were coming from the past and that she could change how she saw her partner. He was just playing out his drama the way he learned it, but she no longer had to play out her role or be in his drama.

Her authentic power emerged. She was able to talk to him directly with honesty, conviction, and courage. She learned to challenge her ego and the father's director voice every time she heard it. With practice, she became more and more authentically powerful in her business and her presentations.

The effect on the company was also dramatic. The staff meetings went better because they became aligned toward the success of the company, instead of playing out dramas from the past.

Beginning to direct from authentic power and becoming proactive rather than reactive are goals for your soul's evolution. The director's voice from the past is not really directing a new performance at all; it is simply directing the same script and lines over and over again. Choosing to consciously direct yourself from the present moment with inner serenity and clear focus is not only empowering to you, it helps others respond more authentically.

Actions and scripts, directed from the inner authority of your higher self, are not dependent on approval from others or on the ego-driven opinions of others. This director has inner confidence and trust in the process from the power of universal energy. The inner spirit directs with a confident voice that can move mountains.

The ego's director is relying on its own power to lead you through your scenes. The ego's power is artificial and is, therefore, being fueled by external and unconscious thoughts and judgments of others. The ego's director listens to voices from the past—causing fear, doubt, and worry.

When you are listening to a voice that causes you to feel anything other than peace, love, and respect for others, you can be sure you are listening to the ego.

THE SCRIPT

In any drama, there is always a script that designates the lines each character gives in various scenes, and the script describes the actions and interactions. On the workplace stage, the script contains a certain language that people understand.

The language becomes part of the culture and is used to help one fit in and be "in the know." Each industry and business has its own cultural vernacular and nuances, in addition to the general business language. The past decade has ushered in the advent of the computer and the Internet; a whole new language emerged.

As part of my consulting experience, I learn the new vocabulary and scripts. For example, the people being served could be clients, patients, citizens, consumers, patrons, customers, members, or investors. The product could be service, money, food consumables, produce, materials, art, entertainment, education, or a number of other things.

I find it interesting how many workplace scripts and lines include words that are actually military combat terms. Scripts include dialogue such as:

- "Launch an attack."
- "Defeat the competition."
- "Going in for the kill."
- "Guerilla marketing."
- "Strategic mission and tactical plan."
- "Working in the trenches."
- "Calling out the troops."
- "Corporate warfare."
- "Damage control."
- "Gathering the arsenal."

I believe this is just a reflection of the competitive and battling atmosphere of businesses today. Competition has increased between businesses; but more significantly, this has also created increased competition among people within a company.

Comparing yourself with others usually creates more envy and antagonism. Then add to it the individual scripts coming from each person within an organization.

The scripts include lines used to communicate the unconscious motives. The lines are memorized from having been used again and again by the characters or players within past melodramas.

You can sometimes recognize an unconscious script in yourself and others when you hear the lines and words that are repeated verbatim in different conversations.

Dave, a marketing executive in a large company, has had the same complaint or critical description of several previous companies in which he worked. "Those guys [the other managers] have no drive. Why don't they work as hard as I do? What's the matter with them? I outperform everybody . . . and I never get a thanks."

He has failed to see that his script is always about him pitted against everybody else. He is the righteous one. His disdain for the other co-workers is felt. Although he is respected for his marketing abilities, he is not liked very much by anyone. Nor is he trusted.

His script is the same with different companies and people, directed by his ego. I mentioned this to him and for the first time, he noticed it for himself. Not without some denial and defenses, I might add.

Admitting there seemed to be a script led him to look behind his ego's direction and discover why his script is always the same. He is working on discovering his hidden, unconscious motives, and also challenging himself when he starts to go down that same path with the similar never-changing script.

Noticing the script and then following that thread or pattern, linked to an earlier period, is helpful. If you are honest with yourself and courageous enough to look for your deeper motives, you can find insight to your script and your director's voice. Through that experience, you can allow your authentic voice to emerge.

GIVING UP THE DIRECTOR AND SCRIPT COMING FROM THE EGO

Perhaps it is time to try another way of operating and begin aligning yourself with spirit and authentic power, instead of the insistent voice of the ego. The script is always the same, leading to the same ending, filled with confusion and usually misery.

Why put your trust in the direction of the ego?

Although the ego tries valiantly to make you look good and protect you from its imagined fears with the "right" dialogue and dramatic lines, it is also a traitor. Your ego says things to you that you wouldn't allow anyone else to say.

Because your ego lacks any real power or self-worth, it will secretly remind you of your weaknesses. The ego is a harsh critic. It is condemning, shaming, and self-effacing. It limits you and keeps you from following your inner purpose by pointing out obstacles and reasons to have doubt and fear.

Your ego will then counter this attack on you with support, justification, and rationalization for your fledgling self-esteem. It truly believes in the drama, which is a fearful recreation from the past. The director from the ego will, therefore, do everything to warn you of the impending danger. And finally, the ego offers to protect and defend you from harm. If you trust in this false claim of safety, you will remain in the drama endlessly.

Scripts allow a person to stay asleep and not be present to the moment. They require little attention to the interaction occurring. Your ego is actual listening to a prompter so you will know when to spew forth the lines from the past. Scripts do not oblige you to listen to another. They allow you to sleepwalk through your life.

So practice listening deeply to others when they are speaking. This involves focusing on another's actual words and not listening to your own internal dialogue. We rarely do this. It takes commitment and constant attention. It also demands that you wake up and operate in the present.

It is not a sin to follow the direction of the ego, but it is a delay in peace and happiness for yourself. If you really knew and believed this, you would stop taking your dialogue from the ego, and choose joy and freedom that the higher self offers.

Listening to the voice of the director coming from the ego is so automatic that it takes great effort to stop yourself. But pay attention to that voice commanding the action of the scenes.

Begin to gently ask yourself the following:

◆ Who is speaking here?
◆ Where have I heard that voice before?
◆ What will happen if I don't follow this direction?
◆ What is the fear behind this direction?
◆ Have I said these lines before?
◆ Is this a rerun of a past scene?
◆ Am I really listening to what another is saying?
◆ Has this script ever worked before?
◆ Is it perhaps time to have a new script?

As you start questioning the voice of the director and script or dialogue in the interaction, you will make room for your authentic voice, from your inner power, to come forth. When you discover the patterns of action and script you have been following, it will seem so glaringly obvious that you will wonder how you didn't notice that you were only starring in reruns.

It is easier to see others' scripts. In fact, others' patterns and scripts may seem quite transparent to you. Recognizing your own takes more honesty and willingness to look behind your starring role and director's voice. But the inner confidence you find will be well worth the effort. You may even reach the point where your script is laughable.

The ceaseless conversation of the ego is ever present. The chatter and commands of the director drown out the "still, small voice" of spirit. The authentic voice will take you to new episodes of creativity and joy, if you allow it to surface.

Finding your inner authority takes waking up to the present and allowing stillness to enter your mind. It demands reclaiming your inner serenity, even in the midst of a dramatic scene. It involves a commitment to maintain alertness, instead of the tired path of the ego.

Your ego would rather sleep through life than allow an assault on your belief system.

Picture a very drowsy little child sitting up in his high chair or stroller. His little eyelids keep dropping shut, but he jerks awake at a sudden sound or nearby movement. He wants to fall asleep.

The ego is that child wanting to sleep rather than to challenge the long running drama. It takes great effort to wake up—but it is time.

Your authentic inner voice often asks you to give up or let go of something your ego believes it needs. It may instruct you to do this:

- ◆ Give up needing to prevail or triumph over another.
- ◆ Give up needing to be superior.
- ◆ Give up needing approval of others.
- ◆ Give up the familiar path and take "the road less traveled."
- ◆ Give up being the victim.
- ◆ Give up roles and definitions of self and others.
- ◆ Give up trying to fix or change others.
- ◆ Give up blaming others.
- ◆ Give up "center stage."

The joy you will experience when you take direction from your inner spirit cannot be compared to the shallow artificial happiness in the ego's drama.

As you practice and demonstrate this to yourself, you will bring forth new responses from both yourself and the others still in the drama. This is how you unhook from the web of interacting scripts and dramatic episodes. This is how you begin to bring light to the stage.

CHAPTER SEVEN

The Camera:
The Lens and Filter of Judgment

The camera of the tragedy in the workplace is actually the most important component of the entire performance. It is the lens and filter through which you view the drama. It comes from you and only you. It is simply an opinion, coming from your ego, but seems real to you.

The camera is judgment, your decision of how to view the world. It comes from your small perspective, based on your past experiences.

Judgment is the *source of all the illusory drama* and consequential problems in the workplace and in your life. Judgment and forming opinions are the ego's method for creating the tragedy that stems from the past, but is being relived in the present.

Wisdom is often said to come with age. This is because a long life provides you with different opportunities and experiences to view life and observe people from different vantage points. The problem with the ego is that it sees its point of view or judgment as the only true and right one.

We need to expand our scope and see life from a higher perspective.

It is as though we are walking down a winding road and we can't see where we are going or what lies beyond, so we create an image in our mind of what we think it will be like, based on the road that we have already traveled.

If we could lift up and look down from a bird's-eye view, we would suddenly see from horizon to horizon. We wouldn't have to make up the scenery or the journey. We would see in all directions. Giving up judgment and opinions is much like rising up and seeing the bigger picture.

If we can expand our experience and our understanding by having an open mind, we will grow in our authentic power that comes from our higher self. But if we insist on maintaining our tiny conclusions, we can be sure they are coming from our ego. We can also be sure that the future will be just more scenes from the past.

A good way to see clearly how we judge and hold on to our opinions is to observe teenagers. Watching their behavior will give us a glimpse of how firmly the ego attaches to its opinion.

If you have ever interacted with a teenager, you have seen that the teen "knows everything." The teenager will fight to be right and is totally closed to the advice of the parent or other adult. The teen will not give up opinions without a battle. Teens want to win at all costs. They do not have the perspective of experience and time. Teenagers are not very open-minded, we could say.

Unfortunately, many adults have strongly held beliefs and opinions, and are unable to hear any other points of view. A conflicting idea or opinion from another is too threatening to the ego.

The ego cannot stand the perceived assault on its beliefs and judgments because the ego actually believes its opinions represent who you are. The unwillingness to hear another point of view comes from the deep insecurity of the ego.

Your ego is afraid of exposure and being caught "wrong."

THE EGO'S CAMERA

The drama that is taking place in your workplace is viewed through your ego's camera, which ultimately censors and filters all the action.

Identifying the significance of the camera to the play is necessary because judgment is so pervasive in all of us that we don't even know we are doing it.

The lens and filter on your camera that colors your view of the drama is judgment, based on your history and experiences with significant people. Most often this includes parents and other influential people in your early childhood. It is, therefore, not real and yet it will affect your current stage— if there are unresolved pains.

The past is a memory. Viewing the stage through your camera will make the past come alive again, on this new stage.

A judgment of another person is simply assigning that person a role in your drama that benefits your ego. The roles you have assigned people are not, of course, the roles they believe themselves to be playing. When you judge other people, you are basing it on your narrow perspective or "small corner of the world."

Other people have their own version of their role and the plot of their story. Because you have assigned them their roles based on your drama, regardless of what they say or do, you will usually still see and hear your expectations from previous scenes.

Even if others don't deliver the lines you assigned them, your lens will be "filtered" by your ego, and you will see and hear what you anticipated.

RECOGNIZING JUDGMENT

Trying to change this dynamic requires, first of all, acknowledging that you are judging others.

As you become aware that you do judge, then you can also start to realize that it is just your opinion. But discovering that it is simply an opinion opens you to the possibility that you could be wrong. Perhaps you are wrong. Just considering the prospect that you might be mistaken is an opening for change and a new perception. That is a big step!

Secondly, you need to recognize that you have interpreted the actions of others in a way that confirms your expectations, which is also a judgment. This step is also very difficult.

The ego finds "not knowing all the answers" hard to accept because your ego has been using its expectation of others to confirm its belief system for a very long time. Interpreting another's actions to meet your ego's needs is such an unconscious, automatic process that it takes persistent and deliberate focus to recognize it and then to challenge it.

Thirdly, you have to admit to yourself that, by keeping the judgment in place, you get the satisfaction of "being right." And of course, "being right," to the ego, is one of the strongest motivations and reinforcements for its existence. By being right, the ego attempts to convince itself that it is really powerful. In reality, however, the ego is still powerless.

Unfortunately for you, the ego's way of always wanting to be right has a huge consequence—the loss of love, peace, and joy in your life. You win the battle and lose the war.

You isolate yourself as your condescension and judgment drives others away. The need to be right and to win is so strong that you won't even see that you yourself are the cause of your own isolation. You will see yourself as the victim of this sad situation and not the cause.

When you can recognize and acknowledge this process of denying your participation in the drama, you are taking a gigantic step forward in the advancement of your soul. This leads to the discovery of your authentic power.

Giving up judgment of others is one of the most difficult lessons in human dynamics because judgment is the automatic and unconscious viewpoint, the lens and filter through which the ego sees the stage and drama.

Judgment in the workplace keeps people from trusting one another. Judgment operates from fear.

When you judge others, you are seeing in them what you cannot face in yourself. The more judgmental and critical you are of yourself, the more judgment you project outwardly. Those harshest with themselves are the most disapproving of others.

Judgment flows from a perception of what your ego believes is the way the world operates. But your ego does not have enough information to know how the world really functions.

Judgment is as though you see someone's toe through a doorway and think you know what the whole person looks like. It is like having a Cocker Spaniel and believing you know what all Cocker Spaniels are like.

Judgment is taking a small piece of information and making an assumption or opinion that you know everything else. It is ludicrous, but your ego convinces you that it is the truth. You live your life as though your beliefs and interpretations are real. They are not. But you frequently cling to them with tightly gripped fists and refuse to let them go.

The lens and filters in your camera prevent you from seeing anything clearly. You do not have a wide-angled lens. Nor do you have a high enough vantage point because you are down amidst the drama on the stage.

It is so difficult to shoot your scenes with any accuracy concerning the reality of what is occurring on your stage. And yet that is what you do. You then accept this blurred and undeveloped image of the world.

The biggest problem with your camera is not just the camera. The difficulty in focusing on the performance accurately is that you do not have enough light to actually view the drama.

Illuminating the stage is what this book is intended to help you do. The universal energy is available for your stage lighting but you prefer the artificial light of the ego. Connecting to that luminosity and spiritual force is the way to finally see clearly into the source of your drama.

The ego cannot connect to spirit anymore than plastic can connect to electricity. Every time you rely on the ego or someone else's opinion, you short circuit your spiritual connection.

Your inner spirit can adjoin with the universal energy and provide a conduit to the power and creativity that supersedes anything you have ever achieved. This light within will brighten as you give up the ego's unquenchable needs and ceaseless judgments. As you surrender your ego to your authentic self, you will discover liberation and enlightenment.

Judgment by the ego causes so many problems on the stage at work, as well as all other stages of your life, that it is amazing that you continue to side with it. It limits your life by creating problems where none exist.

Judgment obscures communication and alienates others because your ego will not allow for any point of view besides its own.

WHY DO WE JUDGE?

Why do we make judgments so rapidly and with such limited information?

The answer is that we are afraid of others, and we are terrified to ask questions. We just jump to our own conclusions rather than delve further. We are fearful that the answers will reveal that we are worthless. So we make assumptions and then carry out our unconscious plot and motives that prove we are the victims.

We hear what we expect to hear, based on the script we assigned the people we cast in our drama. We believe our own script, and we do not let others interfere with the performance—even at the expense of our own happiness.

What are we afraid of?

The sad truth is that we are afraid of being judged by others as not valuable. We are scared to speak up and to be authentic because our ego tells us that we will be rejected. Rather than ask questions and clarify what others are saying to us, we make up our own lines for them.

Because we are judgmental, our own judgment causes us to see others as judgmental, and then we project that on everyone we meet.

After not communicating our feelings to others, we then expect them to read our minds, understand our reactions, and applaud our dramatic performance. We believe our self to be the victim of the attack from lines that they never even delivered.

And then, we wonder why they don't respond to our pain and suffering when we forgot to give them the script!

We judge everyone from the position of our ego and our starring role.

To demonstrate this, think about what happens when you enter a large room with lots of people. First, you judge them on whether you think they like you, respect you, admire you, want to talk to you, already know you, remember you, wish they knew you, hate you, condemn you, value you, trust you, or any number of other attitudes you want them to express about you.

Secondly, you then judge them for their initial and observable characteristics and how they relate *to you*. Are they better looking, smarter, more talented, more confident, inferior, fatter, thinner, better dressed, sexier, more articulate, poorer, older, younger, better, worse, funnier, taller, shorter, wittier, etc. than you?

Then you begin sizing them up, based on your past experiences. Your ego starts casting them in your drama. They don't even know they are auditioning!

Do you know why they don't know they are auditioning for your drama? Because they are all doing the same thing that you are doing: auditioning you and others for their own drama!

Did you know you were trying out for a role in their play?

Your ego sets about creating an image of itself that it wants to project to others. It evaluates and interprets all the other characters and what their roles are going to be. For your drama, your ego does not need any further information because it believes it has enough experience from the past to recognize all the characters on the present stage.

Your ego will even suppose it knows how others think and feel. What arrogance the ego has!

Harry was a high-level manager in a large company that was showing losses in the past quarter. There were rumors of downsizing. One day, as he was walking on the administrative floor, he saw some directors from the company emerge from an executive session that had been going on for several hours. Three of them stopped and were quietly talking in the hall.

As Harry walked by, they seemed to stop talking and nodded grimly at him when he passed by. Harry felt a sinking feeling and went home that night to tell his wife he was probably going to be let go and should start getting his resume together.

His wife was very upset because she didn't work and they had a wonderful lifestyle that she didn't want to see change. The next few weeks or so were going to be a very depressing time for them.

That same morning, shortly after Harry had left the floor, Bob, the vice president of the sales department, came down the same hall. He was feeling good because he had lined up some major accounts that he knew would really help the company recover from the reported losses. As he passed the same three directors, they looked at him and nodded when he passed.

Bob felt a sense of pride, knowing they probably were discussing what a great job he was doing for the company and how he was saving them from any more financial disaster. Bob felt certain he would be getting a promotion and probably a bonus at the end of the year for his great and fruitful efforts in generating revenues for the company.

Interestingly enough, the three directors were actually discussing an upcoming golf round that they were going to play that afternoon. The last quarter had been tough but things were looking up for the company, and they all were feeling good about *themselves and their powerful roles in the leadership* of the company. Neither Harry's nor Bob's names had come up at all that morning!

Harry and Bob had not only reached their own conclusions about the conversations they believed occurred that morning, they proceeded to live the following weeks as though their beliefs were reality.

This is a demonstration of the power of the belief system and our ability to create our own reality. We live our lives as though our beliefs are real.

The real question is: whose direction are you going to follow, your ego or your spirit?

Living through the judgmental world of the ego is like living in a tiny little house with the blinds pulled tightly shut. You do not let the light of day shine into your small and enclosed environment. The ego is fearful that you will discover that you don't need this identity, so it must keep the light from shining in and waking you up from this drama.

Another reinforcement for judgment from your ego is that it gives the ego a false sense of superiority.

Through your camera and lens, you can view yourself and others in any light you choose to validate the story line that you are following. The ego doesn't actually even need the supposed enemy to agree with its opinion. If it wants you to see yourself as a victim, for example, you will believe that it is true even if others don't substantiate it.

The ego will see others as the cause of your pain. If the others don't know it or carry out the same script, the ego will lead you to people who will give you agreement and corroborate your story. In fact, these alliances, based on reinforcing the identity and motives of the ego, are the most common kind of "friendships."

The bond that ties them is the mutual support of each other's drama. They are not authentic friendships.

True friendships are rare.

The combination of judgment and fear of others prevents most people from being authentic in their communication. A relationship between two people is most honest when their authentic selves communicate from the spirit in one honoring and supporting the spirit in the other.

Since most people are operating from the ego and looking for validation of their scripts, relationships based on spiritual honesty are extraordinary and infrequent, at this time, on the planet.

When spiritual relationships do occur, they are very powerful and contain within them the opportunity for transcending the ego world of traps and disillusionment.

Spiritual relationships, wherever they occur, open doors to new worlds of communion with each other and with the awesome spiritual force, bringing peace and satisfaction. These relationships are not easy because they require you to challenge your ego and choose a path that is not familiar. There is usually pain, as well as pleasure, in spiritual relationships.

Not following your ego down its well-worn path requires courage. It may mean that you do not validate people's scripts when they are playing out their ego's drama. But seeing the inner spirit of another is a brave and loving thing to do, especially when the other is in an emotional story of blame or suffering.

Not validating their opinion, which is coming from their wounded ego, takes courage and risk. Your refusal to agree with their story of victimization may cause their ego to react to you with outrage and anger. But your inner spirit and love for them, coming from authentic power, will not allow you to lie or agree with them.

In other words, you do not read the lines in the script that they wrote. Playing out that role for them would actually strengthen their ego, while causing much greater harm to their spirit.

Pete, a warm and loving guy, was carrying out an insane drama with his girlfriend of six months. She was having doubts and fears about the relationship, coming from her early childhood wounds, so she kept giving him mixed messages. She would offer him lots of love and attention for two days, and then withdraw and tell him she needed "alone time" for several days. He was not supposed to call or "suffocate" her during these periods apart.

Pete would be very hurt and disappointed when she would withdraw, after they just had a wonderful weekend or couple days together. He would suffer and wait for her to call and then, when she did, he would try even harder to win her love. He bought her jewelry, took her on trips, and did anything he could to please her.

The push-pull pattern continued with Pete, playing the puppet role, just waiting for her to pull the strings. This was especially hard to watch because he alternated between joy and severe pain. He was "on hold," just waiting to be called back into the dance with her.

In the workplace, Pete was a strong individual in charge of the accounting department for a large construction company. As a CPA, he was not only bright, but also very experienced in the industry. People admired and respected him as a businessman and as an all-around confident person.

Why would he be giving up his power and personal happiness to this woman who it appeared didn't seem to have much compassion for his feelings? His friends would not say too much because of the obvious emotion he was having in this relationship. He would complain, and they would agree with him that it wasn't fair and that it was her fault.

One day, he asked the advice of myself and another lady whom he knew well. I was very proud of Karen when she would not agree with his judgment that he was the victim of the girlfriend's unfair treatment. She said in her southern accent, "Honey, you all must like it. You chose it! If you didn't like it, you all wouldn't keep goin' back for more." Even Pete had to laugh.

Then we discussed how he had given up being the director of his own life, and had handed the whole stage and script to his girlfriend. It was time to start being the authentic director of his life, empowered by his inner spirit. I believe Karen's refusal to validate his story line, based on his judgment from the past, helped turn a light on.

Pete's ego had been playing out scenes from the past of a mother who also had given mixed messages. Of course, it took

Pete more then one momentary glance at the part he was playing in the drama to bring about a change. But he started taking a look at the drama and began to see how he was responsible for his own part in the dynamics of the relationship.

In addition to becoming the director of his own story, as Pete took charge of his life, he also gave his girlfriend freedom to love him without the projection of so much neediness on her. As he needed her less, he gave her the opportunity to love him more.

My wise daughter, Stephanie, who is a very old soul disguised as a beautiful twenty-four-year-old young woman, has dropped many pearls of wisdom to me over the years. When she and her brother, Kyle, were teens, I was so preoccupied with their lives that I, at times, would hardly even go anywhere. I was fearful of the temptations out there for teenagers. I thought I could control things and keep a handle on their behavior if I was protective enough and kept a watchful eye.

My life, during those times, was filled with anxiety, and it was Stephanie's words that helped me let go and trust them more: "Mom, why don't you get a life of your own. Then you wouldn't be worried about Kyle and me all the time."

She was right! My attempt to control the situations, that were out of my control anyway, was making me a prisoner. Even though there were some scathing, nothing-too-serious occurrences, they made it through their teen years fine.

What I can now say to Pete and others who focus their lives on someone else in an attempt to get happiness and security from that person is: "Get a life of your own and be happy." Then you will be the kind of person others will love freely.

We often agree with another's judgment or opinion because our ego wants to be liked and validated. It is easier to agree and lie to people than to answer them honestly if they ask you questions.

I have had to honor myself, and not validate someone's actions and perceptions, when I was feeling hurt. It is not always easy to take a stand for yourself or for someone else when an ego is attacking you. But when you rely on your inner power from spirit, you can withstand the assault from anyone's ego.

Challenging your opinions, which are based on the past and your preconceived ideas about how the world and its people operate, is the way to freedom. When you refuse to limit your world with unfounded judgments, you make way for love and freedom to flow into your life.

Your ego makes the assumption that everyone views life and, in particular, the workplace stage the same. This is absolutely not true. Each person is making judgments all the time and rarely do the interpretations match.

If you can understand that two different dramas and scripts are in play when you have a conversation or especially a confrontation with another, it will help you untangle the confusion.

Peggy was the marketing director for a company that had twelve partners, three offices, and 120 employees. She was dedicated to serving them well, but found it difficult to meet all the needs of the owners. She was having a particularly hard time with a man who seemed critical of everything she did. He frequently told people he didn't even see the need of having her position in the firm.

She came to me and described the fear that she was experiencing in dealing with this person. As she described his behavior, I asked her what she did to meet his marketing needs. She admitted that she did very little. So great was her fear of him and his criticism that she just avoided him.

Because he was a powerful person in the firm, she was having sleepless nights over his dislike of her.

I suggested that it was possible that it was only her interpretation that he didn't like her or didn't value marketing. I asked, "What do you have to lose in trying to get to know him better?" She should see if there were some things she could do to assist him. Peggy was afraid to even approach him, but promised to try.

This story is quite amazing because the whole drama changed as she changed her opinion and fear that he was judging her. She actually was the one judging him and making assumptions.

Peggy forced herself to go to his office and to start gently asking him how she could be helpful to him. She demonstrated caring for his needs and wanting to provide service for his department.

To her astonishment, he started responding by giving her answers and showing interest in the marketing program. She discovered, after a period of time, that his disdain for her was actually stemming from a feeling that she was ignoring him and not interested in helping him with his marketing program.

With time, he became her favorite partner and the fear became a thing of the past. He started volunteering to do marketing activities for the company, such as public speaking and going to community events.

His need for recognition and his judgment of her was pushing her away. Her fear and judgment of him was immobilizing her. When Peggy broke the pattern by giving up judgment, the whole scene changed to one of respect and cooperation.

JUDGMENT CREATES YOUR WORLD

It is characteristic of the ego to make up rules for itself, based on its assumption of the world, and then to try to live by them. Most of these rules are made by your ego's judgment on how you should live your life to prove to yourself and others that you are a worthwhile person.

"Following my rules will make you acceptable and worthy to yourself and to others," says the ego.

These rules are the guidelines and structure in which you perform your role on the various stages of your life. They are the standards by which your ego then evaluates and critiques your performance.

The problem with most of these guidelines is that, since they are made by the ego, they are really just attempts to alleviate self-doubt and fear of inadequacy. It doesn't work because you judge yourself so harshly that you will never be acceptable in your ego's eyes.

This lack of acceptance in yourself leads to projection and lack of acceptance of others.

Finding fault with others becomes a constant way of viewing others through your shadowy filter and lens. It gives you some temporary relief from focusing the camera on yourself, by focusing it on others.

Ed is a very educated and well-read man. He is a lawyer and has learned a lot about critically evaluating all decisions and strategies in all arenas of life.

His keen mind is an asset in the courtroom, and he is a much-sought-after and highly "billable" attorney. His quick ability to ascertain a situation and determine contributing factors has made him an excellent litigator.

Socially, Ed is not so highly esteemed. He has an arrogant nature that seems to come from a very elevated status of himself. He is quick to point out others' faults or frailties. He always knows more about any subject and his conversations are more like lectures than interactive, friendly communication.

His criticism of others is not always blatant, but it is always felt nonetheless. It usually comes as sarcasm or laughter at another's expense. He often puts others down subtly, involving a movie or a show that they might have enjoyed or regarding anything that he deems as beneath his stature or interests.

He is also critical of others not present. He rarely has anything nice to say about anyone. He is quick to point out others' weaknesses and failings. He seems to have a toxic statement about everyone, and he smiles as he dissects others. Finding fault with others gives him an illusory kind of pleasure.

Ed also spends great attention on his own appearance. His clothes are the finest, his shoes are spotlessly polished, and he drives only the most luxurious cars. His jewelry, watches, and accessories are designer labels only; and even his casual look is straight out of a men's fashion magazine. He is perfectly attired, all the time.

In fact, he is pretty much perfect in every way except . . . no one likes him, not even his wife who left him after years of high control and criticism.

What Ed doesn't realize is that his intense criticism and unappeasable attempt to be perfect is belying his incredible disdain and criticism of himself. His attempts at flawlessness in himself and criticism of others are to mask to his own suffering and self-hatred.

He couldn't bear to look within himself at the shame and disgust that he is carrying; instead, he projects all of it outward. His ego has been so terrified that even the incredible pain, that he has gone through in his personal life, has not penetrated it.

You know people like this. Huge fears build huge walls. I don't know what it will take for him to look behind the face of his ego. It takes what it takes!

The goal of this book is to help you put the spotlight on yourself, not with judgment but with a compassionate opportunity to bring the camera into clear focus, allowing you to see clearly. This clarity is worth the effort because it will bring authentic relief to your pain.

Self-acceptance leads to acceptance of others, and this acceptance of others leads to self-acceptance. As you learn one lesson, you simultaneously bring about the other. Self-acceptance is followed by patience with yourself and others. You are also able to find compassion for yourself and show that same caring attitude to others.

The Golden Rule applies here, not as a rule to *try* to follow but as a natural law of cause and effect. What you don't understand is that you can't help but follow it. As you "do unto others," that is *exactly what you do* unto yourself. And "as you do unto yourself," that is *exactly what you do* unto others.

There is no other alternative. You cannot give love and compassion to others, for example, if you cannot give it to yourself. And you cannot give it to yourself if you do not give it to others.

And if what you offer others is harsh judgment, it is because that is also what you offer yourself, and visa versa. Herein lies the closest opportunity to comprehend that "we are not separate."

If you can see this, you will understand Einstein's description that it is an "optical illusion of consciousness" that we are separate. This discovery alone can change your entire life! Right now!

THE FINAL STAGE: JUDGMENT DAY

By now, I hope you are beginning to see that the path of the ego has been one of fear and denial, pain and projection. We might begin to wonder why one wouldn't recognize this as a journey into hell.

Indeed, that is what it is!

Because the tiny, fearful ego is so judgmental of itself and others, it must also project that same judgment onto the all-loving Creator. The ego throughout its life is gradually attempting to build up defenses in preparation for its unavoidable destination—its ultimate fear—that of Judgment Day.

The ego instinctively knows it will never survive after physical death, even though it longs to believe it will go to the everlasting place, the hereafter it wants to enter. And indeed, it dreams of the Promised Land for that very reason, the resting it needs because, quite frankly, the ego is exhausted from all the energy expended in the big chess game of life. The ego has spent a lifetime in the ever-vigilant roles it has created for itself over an entire lifetime.

Of course, the ego is exhausted.

But the ego doesn't believe it deserves heaven. The ego is only an actor and knows it is not worthy of a final resting place of any kind . . . not even in the ground. So the ego sees the point of death, the Day of Judgment, as its greatest fear coming to fruition. As it comes before the Creator, it will finally be found out. The jig is up. It will finally be exposed.

The ego is a fraud.

And from this terrible position, met by the Maker Himself, the only choice, the only justice would be everlasting hell: to have to remain eternally in the pain it has been in all its life, only amplified a thousand times.

The ego will now be with the pain and suffering that it has tried to deny all its life, but it is now its never-ending future. That is justice the guilty ego believes is its only reprisal. That is its just dessert for a job well done of fearing and preying on others for its sustenance.

So says the ego, "Confess your sins. Admit your guilt, so that God will allow you to enter the Gates of Heaven."

That is the final conflict: How can the ego give up its defenses in the face of the Creator, the One who knows how much of a fraud the ego is?

Here, the ego comes face to face with its greatest fear. The fear is so great and so terrifying that all other perceived threats pale in comparison.

Hence, come all the stories of dying if you see the face of God, the fire and brimstone of hell, the whole concept of Judgment Day, and the endless admonitions from the leaders of the churches throughout centuries of fear.

The fear is unconscious, but it is so great that the ego has found ways to attempt to lessen the fear: Confess your sins, do good work, give your money to churches and other worthy causes, and finally, project your guilt onto others. Disconnect from it, go to counselors, take seminars, read the Bible and self-help books. Seek answers to find peace and relief from the pain and stress of living a lie.

But every attempt, even the admirable paths, all lead to fear at some point because the ego knows it will be confronted in the end . . . and then its powerlessness will be exposed.

So once again, the ego plays one more game: it bargains with God.

The ego promises to be good and righteous "if you'll only let me go to Heaven" when time, on the planet, is up. But "good" is a relative term. How good is good enough? How many sins can you commit?

Therein lies the ego's challenge: trying to appear "good" enough for God, but really never measuring up. The ego knows, ultimately, that it is not worthy.

So the fear encountered, which unconsciously resides within every soul, is a pain deeply embedded in the psyche. There is no escape. Hell becomes a reality because it isn't someday—it is now!

Life is a living hell for the ego.

Moments of clarity and joy occur, but the massive consciousness of the ego's world is so great that it is difficult to not be swallowed by it in almost every step of the way.

So where is the door out of this painful maze of self-deception and fear?

The only possibility is in opening the door that has never seen the light of day, the door that the ego has locked shut and thrown away the key. But the key is right here. You must have the courage to challenge your ego, your false self-created identity, that has never given you anything but pain and exhaustion.

You have the key. Great teachers like Jesus, Ghandi, the Buddha, and other spiritual leaders cannot give it to you. They can only point the way.

The way home points back to yourself: the judge, the jury, and the warden of your self-imposed prison.

Only you can set yourself free. You challenge the seemingly powerful ego to finally give up the battle, surrender to the incredible inner spiritual greatness that lies beneath the shabby imitation of your true self.

It takes great attention, it requires fearless dedication, and it demands focus and awareness in the present moment of every passing day. You are waking up from a deep, deep sleep and the desire to go back to sleep is almost overwhelming.

You must fight the urge to sleep by challenging the ego's attempts to hook you, to make you believe it is real, to lead you back down the familiar path of eternal pain and misery. The process would be extremely difficult if it wasn't so powerfully reinforced by your soul when you challenge the ego.

Your soul wants you to awaken.

Many of you are now trying to wake up because the terror and demons of the nightmare are becoming too painful and unbearable. And just as a nightmare wakes you out of a sound sleep, so can a crisis or painful experience wake you up from the ego's dream. Or you can decide right now to wake up, to be restored to your true identity and beautiful soul that you are.

WAKING UP NOW

Isn't it time to let up? Isn't it time to let the light of peace, love, and acceptance shine onto your stage at work and in your life?

People everywhere are tired of this exhausting dance. And one by one, as we shine light on the stage of the ego, it will begin to penetrate the misery and web of pain with the radiance of acceptance and appreciation of each other, as well as ourselves.

We can create an environment of trust and compassion by giving up judgment of others and ourselves.

Because judgment is held by so many, it is difficult to see that it is not real. Mass agreements will only change as we individually give up our own judgments.

How do we do that?

Begin by asking yourself the following questions:

+ Do I compare myself with others?
+ Am I striving for personal glory?

- What are my grievances at work?
- What are my criticisms of the government?
- What are my complaints about society in general?
- What wouldn't I want others to know about me?
- What do I find most unacceptable about myself?
- What about my appearance am I most critical of?
- What do I most mistrust in people I work with?
- Do I know what someone is going to say before they say it? How could I?
- Can I learn to ask questions for clarity instead of make assumptions?
- If I were to meet my Maker today, what would I fear would be my worst sin?

Looking at the answers to these questions will actually tell you about the source of your judgments and help you recognize how you judge yourself and others.

It is time to start challenging your ego's threatened opinions.

It is not a sin to follow your ego's direction, but it always delays your path to enlightenment. It takes watchfulness and concentration to notice the slightest thoughts and irritations that are the seeds of judgment. Not allowing them to grow into full-blown judgments is the best thing that you can do. Snapping them off at the roots and weeding the garden frequently will keep it free from the overgrowth of weeds that would take over the sun and sustenance that belongs to the healthy plants.

As your awareness grows, you will be amazed at how many times during the day you make judgments or form immediate perceptions of others. By letting go of these opinions as quickly as they occur, you will cause them to dissipate and, in their place, you will feel and see the radiance, beauty, and joy that are your natural inheritance.

You will replace your negative emotions through giving up judgment with a new, softer feeling of respect, love, and compassion. The feelings of the heart will rush in to fill the void caused by the release of judgment and prejudice. You will see a new, brighter, freer world as you continue to resist judgment, day by day.

Your continued success in resisting to make judgments will reinforce this new way of being. You will become strong and detached from the outcomes of daily events because no longer will you have a personal agenda attached to them. You will experience an independence you have never known and you will feel physically lighter and more energetic, joyful, and peaceful. Most of all, you will feel released from the weight of being accountable for all the outcomes both at work and elsewhere.

Controlling your world by trying to influence the actions and choices of others will become a thing of the past. You will realize it was an illusion anyway. To give up judgment calls forth your trust in the universe and your innate spiritual integrity. It requires becoming present and giving up the past, which has been dictating the workplace and the world.

Giving up judgment requires the companion ability of trusting that you are not needed to direct the daily drama. It allows you freedom because you are no longer holding yourself responsible.

The drama in the workplace, as well as the world, is comprised of complicated scenes in which you are both judging and participating every day. Therefore, unraveling this multifaceted drama can be complex. So keep noticing your judgments and then ask your inner spirit for help in giving them up.

Dispel them. Unleash your freedom, peace, and joy, which have been enshrouded in clouds of judgment. Just let go.

If you look at the base of judgment, you will see that it is not power. It is fear. And once again, fear is of the ego. So, when you judge, know that you are operating from the ego. You can see judgment in others but not in yourself. Judging is an attempt to weaken or disempower another, even if only in your private thoughts.

Your ego believes if you can discount others, you can hamper or minimize their power to hurt you. But the damage *inflicted on yourself is far greater* than any threat you perceive from others. Allowing them the freedom to just be, accepting them for exactly who they are, is the most loving and enlightened thing you can do.

Understanding how judgment creates your world is the missing link to your freedom from pain and misery.

The ego wants to make others smaller when our work is to empower others, to release them to their true greatness, to help restore them to their real identity. But we cannot do this by diminishing them from the viewpoint of the ego that wants us to be superior to others.

An enlightened leader fans the spark of brilliance in those who are being led into flames of passion and creativity. With judgment, however, the ego-driven leader douses these sparks and puts them out.

As a leader, understanding how you judge others is a most crucial lesson. You can't help those you lead through your ego's eyes. You help them without the ego.

UNIVERSAL LOVE

Universal love is the source of all energy and light.

Love lights the world. It shines on everyone, and opens hearts and minds to the beauty of creation. Love radiates like the sun, a joyous expression of the magnificence of our spiritual essence. It recognizes that all is well and that nothing needs to be changed.

But if love is the sun, judgment is the cloud that obscures it. By clearing away the clouds, by clearing away judgment is the way to freedom of expression and the ability to receive love, joy, and inner contentment in your life.

So powerful is love that it disarms and melts away the ego's falseness. Love, in its purest form, unhampered by judgment, cuts through all the ego's negativity.

Seeing others as enemies is a result of judging; you see their actions as causing your feelings. Holding others responsible for your feelings is a gigantic misperception. When you begin to see how judgment permeates and colors your entire world, you will begin to see that it also destroys your peace and harmony.

Judgment is so persistent that giving it up will take focus and constant attention. But the results will reward you a thousand-fold.

You will see the world differently when you release judgment. You will stop holding others responsible for anything. You will enjoy the beauty of the human experience and receive the rewards for helping elevate understanding and compassion. As you practice your new insights by demonstrating to others and yourself that you accept them as they are, you will become an enlightened and powerful leader.

One of the greatest results of giving up judgments of others is that you simultaneously give up judging yourself. This love and acceptance of yourself is freedom at the ultimate level. It is your ego's self-loathing and fear that created the whole drama to begin with. It is the ego's lack of self-worth that directs the drama in order to deny its fear.

Here is your freedom!

Can you see that it is through the practice of giving up judgment that you will become authentically strong, whole, and complete? Giving up judgment will remove the barriers that prevent you from being all that your heart desires. If you really trusted this information, why would you not give up judgment right now?

As a leader, when you practice doing this, you will make a tremendous difference in the workplace and the world. You will be recognizing the spirit in yourself and in others that will create a new level of communication, inspiration, and success in the workplace. You will have the inner joy of helping enrich the lives of others as well as yourself.

CHAPTER EIGHT

The Enemy (Antagonist) and the Conflict

The drama in the workplace would not be complete without the role of the enemy playing a major part.

The enemy is the root of all your troubles, so believes the ego. The enemy causes the ego unbearable pain and incredible fear. The enemy, therefore, must be dealt with to diminish or to completely remove the suffering. This is done by destroying the cause—the ego's enemy.

There may actually be more than one enemy. But even with several enemies at once, the dynamics are always the same.

Throughout literature, antagonists exist but the heroes usually emerge the victors when pitted against their formidable opponents. The ego believes it must face challenges also and always claim victory. The alternative is to surrender and that is humiliating to the ego.

If the opponent appears to the ego to be mightier or more powerful than you, it will engender great fear, indeed. So central to the drama is the enemy in the workplace that your ego can cause you to become obsessed with and often even immobilized by the intensity of the threat that you believe is coming from the enemy. Your ego may direct you to hours of suffering and anguish over how to deal with the situation.

The enemy is usually seen as a threat to the ego's security and well-being.

However, many times the enemy is the source of pain because of the ego's envy of that which the enemy has or has attained. It could be status, material wealth, beauty, or any number of external things that your ego covets.

Jealousy has been the root of battles between individuals, families, communities, and even nations throughout history.

The source of major dramas and even death is the jealousy or fear of losing the beloved to the enemy. The eternal triangle has been the motive and story line of incredible pain and jealousy for centuries. The "wrath of a woman scorned" represents this passion played out due to jealousy. Men have dueled and fought wars over the woman they loved.

The intense passion and misery over the beloved is because the attachment, formed in the love relationship, offers the most opportunities for joy as well as pain. Unrequited love or love lost have been the most painful experiences for humans throughout history. However, even these dramatic and sad situations can offer healing and new understanding if those involved choose to learn the lessons.

To understand this more fully, let's look at how human beings have responded to the enemy or the "other" who is a threat to the welfare of individuals and societies throughout history.

Cave men found weapons to defend themselves and provided security for themselves with the threat of force. In the Middle Ages, people built castles with high walls, moats around them, and drawbridges for protection from the enemy. Early settlers in America, traveling in wagon trains, circled the wagons for protection; then they built forts with high walls and lookouts to keep the enemy at bay and keep those inside safe and secure.

In modern times, nations battle in the name of national security and have departments of defense to orchestrate military combat to ensure their country's safety.

But when does the defense become the offense?

Humans, on an individual basis, both in the workplace and other environments, build walls and defenses to protect themselves. These ego-defense mechanisms are boundaries that your ego believes will keep you secure and protected.

But these protective walls are most often barriers to communication.

Your ego wants to keep its belief system in place. In addition to its ego-defense mechanisms, the ego also develops its team of allies to help combat the enemy, just as nations do in wars. The alliances, formed with individuals that you find to agree with your viewpoint, are bases on the bond against a common enemy.

In the workplace, I have seen people, who do not even like each other, come together when it supports their belief in the enemy. They believe there is power in numbers. Having allies helps fortify the artificial power of the group that is battling a common opposition. But this group is actually operating from fear. This is the basis of labor unions.

The chain of actions and reactions to the perceived threat from one another can grow to horrendous proportions. When it is large groups, it becomes unwieldy and the intensity can be overwhelming to those participating in the conflict. When nations see each other as enemies, war is the result.

So who is your enemy in your workplace?

The irony of the drama around the enemy is that different people view different "others" as the enemy. The enemy is created by the ego, based on its viewpoint. Who you deem worthy to be your opponent is the one who is the biggest threat to you and your personal security.

In my work with various companies, it is always so clearly evident that each individual is the star in his or her personal drama and the enemy is, therefore, cast by that individual.

For example, several people may tell me that a particular person is the source of the problem in one department or at a certain level. But several more have an opposite viewpoint or at least do not share the same enemy. Then I talk to one of the word-processing people, for example; and she is oblivious to the names, mentioned by the others, but is certain the real enemy is the other word processor by whom this person feels most threatened.

If the person whom you view as an enemy is in a higher position than you in the workplace, the threat will seem more intense because of his or her perceived power. But even then, you can learn to deal with the fear and have an authentic conversation if you understand the dynamics.

Fear and the sense of separateness are currently barriers to authentic communication.

If people weren't so terribly miserable, these dramas would be almost laughable because the enemy is so clearly an illusionary creation, all based on viewpoint and perception. Human beings are so separated from their spiritual source that they see themselves separate from each other as well.

The creation of enemies is the result of personal fears of the ego being projected outwardly, assigning the part of antagonist to the one who is most fearful in your own personal drama.

The ludicrousness of this belief of separateness from our fellow human beings with the resulting creation of the "enemy" is most clearly illustrated in examples in our recent world history. Russia, who was considered an enemy of the United States, was suddenly recast and instantly the country was no longer the enemy after decades of a Cold War.

When I was twenty years old, I traveled through Europe and we stayed a few days in Germany with a relative of one of my traveling companions. He had been a German Panzer officer. My father had been a World War II pilot and had been a POW in Germany for nine months. This man and I saw the tragedy and unbelievable insanity of war, as we realized he and my father would have killed each other and did kill each other's countrymen during that war. And now, I was his house guest. What changed?

FIGHT OR FLIGHT

When a human being is feeling threatened, the instinctive response of fight or flight is often triggered. The ego will make this decision in a flash because the ego cannot operate from a calm and serene place. It cannot stand an attack on its belief system, so it reacts immediately.

In battle, the troops retreat when the enemy is too strong; they wave the flag of surrender. Animals will fight, unless they see that the opponent is too fierce to overcome and then they retreat. This fight-or-flight syndrome is universal.

However, in the drama of the ego, the retreat has become a way to avoid facing the fears of the ego. Retreat can come in the form of refusing to have further conversations, an impasse. It can include shutting oneself off in a closed office. One can even leave the current stage for a better opportunity.

However, if the lesson or opportunity presented is not learned, the drama will follow. Giving up or giving in to isolation is acknowledging you have no power. But it is only the ego who is powerless and it is the one who needs to hide or escape.

So you may just leave a situation, not even consciously knowing that it is fear driving you away.

The power and strength of the ego's thought system are demonstrated by the desire to escape feeling pain by leaving fearful situations. Denial is the tool used by the ego to protect itself and keep fear below the surface, where it does not have to be acknowledged. Denial is such a powerful tool that you don't even know it is occurring.

Lyle was a partner in a firm that was aggressively growing and expanding its client base. There was often a lot of competition among the partners, and each partner's compensation was based on their incoming revenues. This competitive environment did nothing to help the partners come together and work as a team.

Lyle was feeling pressure to build his department, so he became passively combative with the other partners. He tried to assert his weight in decisions that he felt helped his position in the firm. He was very skilled in his articulate arguments, and he usually was able to put others down with a disguised sarcastic remark that carried a zinger for the recipient.

What other partners didn't know was that Lyle was operating from fear. His passive attacks were followed by retreats. One way he retreated was, when in a confrontation in which he started to feel threatened, he would say to his opponent, "Well, I'm not going to argue with you."

This left the other person feeling shut down because saying anything in response would be confirming that this was an argument. Lyle would the leave the conversation, close his office door, and be relieved that he didn't have to receive any more attacks. His door was actually closed most of the time and his "shut out" mode kept people away, unless he chose to come back into the group. This passive attack, followed by a retreat, was unknowingly causing Lyle more harm than safety.

Other forms of retreat, such as silent treatments or pouting, occur in various environments. These scenes sometimes remind me of children in the sand box, throwing sand, hitting each other with shovels and pails, and then finally retreating into the corner. "I'll take my toys and leave," says the ego.

I had a relationship with a man that I cared very much for. Because of the intensity of the relationship, we would unknowingly bring up each other's issues, much like a mirror to each other. What was disappointing to me was that we could not seem to break through to direct communication. Whenever the conversation brought up his hidden fears, his response was, "Oh, ple-e-ease. Don't go there." He would then shutdown and refuse further conversations.

He described to me that he and his former wife had similar conversations, and he wasn't going to ever do that again. "You sound like Mary Ann!" he told me. This was his passive attack on me—casting me in the role of the ex-wife, also known as the enemy. I never knew what would have happened in our relationship because he "wouldn't play" if the dialogue didn't fit his script.

We had many wonderful times together, but he wouldn't allow the block that kept coming up to be penetrated. I finally had to take a stand for myself and tell him that I was unwilling to continue in a relationship that cast me as the enemy. I couldn't walk on eggs to fit into his ego's script.

The question to ask when you are isolating, fleeing, not speaking to someone, shutting down, or using any form of flight is: "What am I fleeing from?"

It is not other people who you perceive as the enemy. It is a fear within you—a fear that they merely trigger with their words or actions. This is where the ego does not want to look, so it places the cause with people.

When flight or isolation is not chosen as a response to a threat from a perceived enemy, the other reaction is to defend with a fight. The *need* to defend is the key here.

If you would gently look behind your ego's need to defend, you would begin to discover what is holding you hostage and keeping you hostage is fear. The moment you feel defensive is the exact second you should look *within* for the cause. But your ego will not let you.

Defense is the ruling force in the ego's world because to look at what lies beneath the surface would put an end to the ego. It would be liberation.

Defensive reactions occur in varying degrees of intensity, depending on the size of the issue that ego is denying. The greater the defense, the greater the fear and the stronger the false belief system.

Whether you are choosing fight or flight in a confrontation with an enemy, you are still being driven by the ego. There is something deep within you that you have hidden from yourself, and you believe defending or fleeing will keep you from having to look at it.

GUILT AND SHAME

One reason it is hard to confront your fears and to allow them to emerge is that there is guilt associated with all the pain the ego is trying to cover up. Your ego fears that if this secret is exposed that you will be shamed.

There is a hidden core belief beneath the surface that is self-defacing and disgraceful. Your ego believes that there is something so reprehensible about you that you cannot accept or bear to look at it.

If you only knew that by facing your fear would allow light to shine on it. You would discover its very origin and that would set you free. Freedom would end your need for the defenses, the plots, the battles that your ego thrives on. You would be releasing the grip of the ego from your soul.

But your ego does not want you to be free.

The peace that would come from ending this intense battle would be so profound you would be changed forever. The energy that would flow in, when your little ego was not frantically stirring up drama and defenses, would give over to soft and exquisite serenity. The thrashing and turbulent waves of emotion would give way to the gentle lapping of calm waters. The cloudy storm would subside, and the sun would come shining forth upon the still waters. Literally, that would be the difference.

Who would not choose that quietness and tranquility over chaos and uncertainty, agony and despair?

The ego, that's who. It has you so baffled and disconnected from your source that you believe its incessant direction, so you rarely question that there is another way to see things.

ADDICTIONS

When the ego fails to keep this dissatisfaction and fear of its awful shame buried deeply enough, you become very anxious. It feels to you like a general sense of apprehension and nervousness that is undefined. Some people may actually experience anxiety attacks.

When this internal discontent is at its worst, the ego may attempt other methods besides fight or flight.

The goal of the ego is that it wants you to become numb. It wants to you to remain unconscious at work and elsewhere. If the methods employed already—such as defense, flight, alliances (or gossip), sabotaging, grandiosity, intimidation, blaming, being the martyr, and manipulation—are not keeping you anesthetized, the ego will seek other options.

For example, you may try to render yourself numb with self-medication in the form of alcohol, drugs, and other addictions. Even anti-depressants, prescribed by physicians, are ways to keep the ego from fully experiencing its pain by reducing the uneasiness and self-disgust. These methods, therefore, help the ego avoid its suffering by changing or altering the mood or state of mind.

There are a variety of other "fixes" or mood-elevating methods that are only temporary and are, also, actually capable of becoming addictions. These include gambling, eating, sex, shopping, working, or any frenzied activity that gives a sense of a "high" or mind-elevating, temporary pleasure.

However, the ego becomes insensitive or numb to the "effect" and begins to need more and more of the "drug of choice" to keep the ego's dissatisfaction in check and for the high to continue. So the frequency, intensity, and general amount of the drug needed to attain the satisfaction increases, thus escalating the compulsion for the drug or a need to replace it with a stronger drug. That is the nature of addictions.

Then at some point, the addiction itself becomes the problem, i.e. alcoholism, drug addiction, eating disorder. The pain becomes unbearable for the self and others. As the compulsion for the drug grows stronger, the lack of self-worth intensifies, leading to feelings of desperation and fear.

However, this self-inflicted trap can lead to an opportunity of great advancement through a breakthrough in consciousness, if the individual decides to surrender. The obsession for the drug is running the whole show, and the denial is intense.

But when the painful recognition of the addiction in one's self occurs and the individual finally surrenders, healing is then possible. This is the turning point, such as you see when someone "hits rock bottom" and chooses spiritual growth through counseling or a support group, such as AA or others.

Liz is one of the most accomplished women I know. She has a successful career and still maintains time to do hundreds of other things. She is a fabulous gourmet cook, putting on great parties at the drop of a hat. She sits on a number of boards and seems to be the head of nearly everything she gets involved in.

Her house is spotless, her gardens are always beautiful, and she seems tireless. Her children are grown, but she spends lots of time with her beautiful grandchildren. She belongs to so many groups and has so many activities that she is rarely home.

It has been only recently that Liz has started to notice that something is missing in her life. She is so "busy being busy" that she has little time to be introspective or wonder about the actual quality of her life. Liz just told me that she finally realized that she is terribly lonely. She is truly afraid to stop this frenzied activity for fear she will have to face this fear of solitude and loneliness.

The attainment of inner peace, through being content to be alone, is a necessary part of evolution of the soul. Seeking this busy lifestyle to avoid being in touch with herself and facing her fears is exhausting Liz. What she doesn't realize is the resistance of being alone that is frightening her.

Resistance of the fear and the anticipation of the unknown are causing her deep anxiety and pain. Letting go and facing the fear will bring her new peace. Until she connects with her inner spirit, the many activities and worthwhile accomplishments will not satisfy her soul. They are external efforts to keep her numb and to fill a void of being needed and loved.

Unfortunately, this is not just Liz's story. I know many women like Liz. I also know many men who can't bear to be alone and quiet with themselves.

The ego will block your journey back to yourself with all kinds of external activities and distractions, but the only path to peace and joy is looking within.

Liz is already a step ahead of many people by being aware of her addiction to activity as avoidance of facing herself. She is practicing spending more alone-time and is beginning to feel some relief. She is a witness that the resistance was more painful than the actual doing it.

Letting go, letting go, letting go. How the ego fights it.

The spirit within can use any pain or circumstance to restore itself to its true identity if you sincerely desire to transcend the prison it is in.

Recognizing and recovering from addictions are some of the most powerful ways to spiritual growth and freedom because you have to overcome intense denial that surrounds the fear of being exposed. It takes great courage and trust; but the rewards are freedom, peace, and love.

VICTIM OR ENEMY?

How do you deal with the enemy in your workplace?

First, it takes courage and a willingness to face the unalterable fact that the enemy is only your opponent, based on your casting that person in that role. The ego will fight this vehemently because the ego truly believes the other person is really a threat. Your ego has projected all blame on that person and has cast you as the victim.

The situation with which you are struggling is really not the issue. Its only validity is in your ego's drama: to strengthen or defend itself. Either position is still stemming from fear. Those people, who you believe are causing so much turmoil, may not even know they have been cast in that role. Or they may believe that you are the enemy and that they are the victim!

So the question is: Who is attacking whom?

What appears to be an attack from another is actually their ego defending them from being in their own role as the victim. You think you are the victim, but so do they. You each assign each other the role of enemy and yourself the role of victim. How can this be? But that is what is happening with individuals, groups, companies, communities, and nations.

A large insurance company was falsifying reports and turning down claims from the very people who were paying the premiums to keep them in business. They had people within the company forging doctor's names that disallowed certain procedures and surgeries so they would not have to pay out the expenses incurred for medical charges.

The company was fearful of a negative cash flow position. This fraudulent action of falsely declining claims was a demonstration of frightened egos, accelerating their need to prevail into an offense. The very people they were supposed to protect became the enemy and suffered the consequences.

When it was exposed, the company actually had justified their actions and even in the end, the CEO would not acknowledge his responsibility. He saw himself as the victim and acted amazed that this could have all happened to him.

I had a friend volunteer to help me on an out-of-town project. It was an hour-and-a-half drive and, by the time we would get back, it would be an all-day commitment. I had not requested his help, but he offered and seemed excited to go with me. I was very appreciative and relieved to have his help. Twenty-four hours before we were supposed to go, when it would be difficult to find someone else, he started trying to withdraw his offer.

He asked if I really needed his help because he had some other things that he would "kinda like to do." I said that I really did need him now because it would be too late to get someone new. He sounded irritated but said, rather curtly, that he would be there.

That morning he called again and tried to make a couple more excuses and did say he would be late. One part of me felt like a victim and I was tempted to say, "Just forget it." However, on a deeper level, I knew that his ego had turned me into the enemy, by causing him to do something against his will that was actually just holding him to his word.

I told him that he was trying to make me the enemy. I recognized he was hoping to make me feel guilty but it wasn't working. I joked with him and made him laugh, but I did not let him off the hook that he had put *himself* on. The happy ending is that he later thanked me for expecting the best from him.

He recognized that he had a pattern of making promises in the moment because it made him feel good to offer to help people. Then he would try to back out if something better came along. The way he unconsciously got out of it was to make the other person "wrong" or the enemy. His ego believed that would justify his not keeping his word. I refused to play the role and it forced him to see his own pattern.

THE CLIMAX: FACING THE ENEMY

The point arrives in the drama when the main character/ star must face the enemy. The alternative is to continue suffering or to depart. This moment comes when the star is prepared to take a stand and face what he/she fears.

Now this can result in the ego attacking or confronting the enemy who is perceived to be the threat. This ultimately leads to another continuing drama that escalates with the same enemy, finding a new enemy, or moving to a different stage. Nothing is resolved or learned when one or the other still loses. Between countries this is called a war, and war does not lead to peace.

The blaming of others for your pain or situations is abdicating responsibility for your own feelings or experiences. The problem with doing this is that it gives you no out, no road of escape from the pain. It is a terrible place to be because it appears so hopeless to you, which it actually is not.

Reclaiming your power over yourself, your feelings, and your circumstances allows you to change your mind, to see it differently, and to stop being held hostage by pain or discomfort.

But denying authentic power has enormous appeal to the ego. Its desire to stay in control is so strong that it becomes perpetuating for the ego to blame others.

If you look behind the ego's fear, you will see that only your authentic self is powerful and that others do not have the power to harm you, unless you give them that role. As Eleanor Roosevelt said, "No one can make me feel inferior without my consent."

So the question to ask yourself when you are having a difficult confrontation or series of uncomfortable interactions with someone else is: "What is my perceived threat with this person?"

Even if your emotion toward that person is envy, there is still a perceived threat or fear underneath that emotion.

Secondly, recognize that this person is actually giving you an opportunity to heal yourself from some inner pain lodged in your psyche. This person's presence at work and in your life can lead you to a new freedom and strength if you use it to let go of old fears and the death grip of the ego.

The true victory and, finally, peace are realized when the ego discovers *the only battle is with the self.* It is here that an opportunity to bring about a true armistice occurs. For it is at this point that the ego can choose to recognize that it has fully projected the blame and cause of the conflict unto someone else.

It is important to understand that your reaction is not occurring because of what is happening with this person. The "enemy" in the present circumstance is hooking your ego from a past scene because you have assigned that person a role from your long-ago cast of enemies. It is here that the chance occurs to see other people differently—not as those to serve you in your given role to them as the enemy.

If you or the other character could stop for a moment and see that it is the judgment and subsequent expectation of the other, coming from the ego, that is actually the cause.

But this would require you to step out from behind the face of the ego and to be willing to see that you are equally responsible for the cause of the painful battle with the enemy. The automatic and usual tendency of the ego is to simply project it fully onto the other person, rather than looking at the self, making that person the cause.

And so the ego continues to protect itself, putting the blame outside the self, and seeking reinforcement from others that it is innocent. The ego continues down the path endlessly, seeking relief but traveling in pain.

What is the way out of this dance of pain and suffering?

Stop assigning roles that are followed by expectation, but that can only be done in the present. So start by being in the present moment.

You also need to recognize the dynamics of the egos in this conflicting relationship and acknowledge to yourself what is really occurring. Know that your opponents believe that they are the victim.

You must understand and realize that only by going through the pain can you find the way out. You need to stop resisting the pain and let it fully emerge, so that you can see what it is you are so fearful of. The ego's path has led to nothing but pain and suffering, blame and shame. Why not try this new courageous way to deal with the situation?

You start by turning the focus inward to discover what your own doubts are, so you can stop projecting and blaming the other person. The pains and conflicts between you are actually the very portals to moving to a higher level in the development of your soul and your ability to relate to others without fear.

This effort to recognize your ego's judgments and expectations takes deep concentration. After all, your ego wants you to go back to sleep.

You must focus on this task of recognizing the ego's efforts to control things by casting you as the victim. But the experience itself cannot be done for you.

You must commit to your own spiritual growth. That commitment will lead you out of pain and suffering and bring about the peace you so desire.

So the challenge is to give up being the victim, give up blaming, give up the envy and fear and, instead, place your trust in your inner spirit. That is not easy when your ego is in control. But when you do, the freedom is endless.

Unfortunately, this moment is usually passed by in favor of the ego needing to prevail and to be right.

But step back, just for a moment, and ask yourself the following questions:

- When have I felt this way before?
- When have I faced this enemy before?
- What am I afraid this person can do to me?
- What would happen if I expressed my real feelings?
- Which automatic strategy do I follow—fight or flight? What is the benefit to doing that? What is the loss?
- Whom do I see as my allies? What do they say to strengthen my ego and my script? Can I give this up?
- What is my goal—to win or to be at peace?
- Am I perhaps wrong?

THE ARMISTICE AND FORGIVENESS

As you answer these questions, you will gradually take ownership for the feelings you are experiencing. You will make the slow, but powerful, distinction that you alone are responsible for your feelings.

This is the beginning of independence.

If you have the power to cause the feelings in yourself, then you are also capable of releasing these discomforting thoughts and feelings. The dawning of this profound idea is your means to freedom. Peace resides within you. Only you can allow and actually create the negative and usually fearful emotions to enter.

You are bound to have relationships that cause you stress or discomfort in the workplace. The greater the sense of anxiety created when dealing with the individual, the more powerful the opportunity to heal and rebuild the relationship.

The workplace also provides time and frequent interactions in which to learn and practice this new way of owning your authentic power and changing the relationship to a higher level. As you progress in this process, you will learn to notice even slightest moments of discomfort and learn how to release them before they take hold of you.

It will not be as easy to let go of painful responses and reactions in the intense conflicting relationships. But with time, you will come to know that it works in all situations— from the most emotionally turbulent relationships to the slightly stressful ones.

You will learn to uncover the causes for conflict in the relationships where even no communication is occurring at all. The emotion you are holding is not really caused by the other, only by you.

As you can feel the pain underlying the negative emotion and finally identify the origin that is some situation that occurred in your childhood, you will come to fully realize the current individual is not the root of your pain. The person is simply the mirror helping you remember the beginning of the thought system that you formed as a child to protect yourself.

As you have experiences in the workplace that trigger and cause you to relive emotions of the past, it becomes an opportunity to allow the feeling and reaction to surface so that you can look at it. You will also see that people's behavior is not about you, but is a result of their own thought system.

The tendency to take it personally is profound, but the truth is: it is not personal. It is part of their personal drama, as is yours, and most of all, that it is not real.

When you acknowledge your pain and accept that the source is your own thought system, you will recognize that other people are not guilty and you can forgive them. So whatever the powers that be, at work or at home, the only real power is authentic power coming from your inner, higher self operating from the only real source, that of spirit.

All else is the ego, creating drama to validate itself and

substantiate its existence. Fear and doubt are of the ego and all negative emotions stem from that, whether you recognize it or not.

How do you forgive someone that you have been battling with either silently or verbally?

Forgiveness occurs when you release your claim or desire for victory over another. Forgiveness sets you free because it takes a great deal of energy to hold someone else responsible for your misery. When you see clearly that only you have the power to choose your feelings, forgiveness is close.

The next part occurs when you stop taking it personally when someone else does anything that you perceive as hurtful. Individuals are on their path and are doing what they need for their plan of learning. Your opponents are following their script and you are not the cause of their beliefs or feelings. This is what Jesus meant when He said, "Forgive them, Father; for they know not what they do."

When you are able to look gently behind what the fear or strongly held belief is which is causing the projection to another, the pain will be released and forgiveness is complete.

Finally, self-forgiveness occurs when you can shine that same compassion and love to your own heart, which will release the guilt and original shame that is holding it in place. This is true *absolution*. This is true freedom. An unhealed heart cannot experience love, peace, and joy at work or anywhere else. Therefore, forgiveness is the access to love, forgiveness of self and others.

When you can forgive another, as well as your self, you will have a new form of communication available to you. You will talk from a place of inner serenity, rather than a reactionary and guarded position. Your spirit will recognize the spirit in the other and you will know that you are not separate. You will see the dynamics of conflicted relationships change dramatically.

FOCUSED LISTENING

What will happen when you stop playing out your role and quit assigning others their role?

Recognizing the spiritual essence in other people in the workplace, or anywhere for that matter, is done by recognizing that their egos are not who they are. With focused listening, the leader can begin to hear what the other is really saying.

This can be especially effective at times when the other person is acting out an intense ego drama. It is important here to give feedback that recognizes the inner essence, not the ego's identity.

With practice, you will become better at deep or focused listening. It is more difficult when the other is steeped in a drama or defensive posture that is an emotional or hostile situation, and it takes even more concentration so that your own ego is not hooked.

When we give power to another's belief system, this controls us, but only until we recognize its insanity. That is really all there is to it. It only takes a moment to suddenly see clearly and then it is not long before that is the only way you see. This is true transformation, the true integration of your authentic, spiritual self with your ego role.

And someday, everyone will see the ridiculousness and insanity of the massive game of the ego. That is why *The Course in Miracles* says the world will end in laughter.

Practicing inner serenity, during hostile or fearful situations created by egos in the work force, will help you hear the fear in the other's drama. It is here that you gently ask questions, as one would when speaking to a tiny little baby, that will help the other feel understood and accepted. When the other feels acceptance, the walls of fear can come down more easily.

Since you have been responding to the ego, both to yours and others', for so long, it has become automatic. So practicing inner serenity is crucial. It takes discernment and patience as you learn this new skill.

Developing the quality of deep listening will help you not only free others, but it will free yourself as well. This is a basic and vital step in becoming an enlightened leader.

Disengaging from the ego conversations and dramas requires the following:

- ♦ Feeling the quiet centeredness and inner serenity of being present. This quietness allows you to feel your spirit and keeps you from being hooked by the ego's drama.
- ♦ Recognizing the inner spiritual essence of the other. This allows you to see past the words and actions of the ego.
- ♦ Deep listening and acceptance, so the walls of the other's ego can start to come down.
- ♦ Gently asking questions that will reveal the true needs of the other.
- ♦ Acknowledging and giving feedback to the real self, not the ego.

Wounded people cannot be productive and creative, or reach their full potential. The current workplace environment needs healing. Like a giant machine, it cannot run with faulty parts. The machine will work with integrity when the parts are whole and complete. Restoring individuals in the workplace to their true identities expands the potential of individuals and the company as a whole.

This process of unhooking the drama is most successful when the leaders, who become aware of their own drama, initiate the steps.

It starts with the seeds of recognition that you are more than your ego. A growing sense within you will build, causing your ego to diminish. Every time you give up assigning the role of the enemy to anyone else, your own inner personal power grows.

As your authentic power grows and you are restored to your true identity, you will be able to you help restore others to theirs as well. And this will restore the environment to one of trust, respect, honor, and compassion. In this environment, people will thrive and companies will exceed their goals for success.

PART III

AWAKENING
FROM THE DRAMA

CHAPTER NINE

Enlightened Leadership

THE ENORMOUS CONFLICT

Enlightened leaders operate from their authentic source.

To become that kind of leader means facing the constant challenge coming from the ego. When individuals who are operating from the ego get a glimpse of the truth that they are not the ego or identity that they think they are, an enormous conflict begins between the ego and spirit. The conflict is felt on many different levels and in many different situations.

The ego, of course, wants you to stay asleep and, therefore, any threat to its existence causes it to *intensify its grip* on you.

This conflict is deeply felt, and it is actually so intense that it is easier to go back down the path of the ego, the one of pain and suffering. That is exactly what most people do!

The challenge is to begin to do that which will help you start to wake up from this insane drama of the ego. You must see that an enormous conflict within yourself occurs when you begin to face the ego and its complex web of control. The ego is attempting to keep you starring in your melodrama and tragedy.

Choosing to align yourself with the ego or align yourself with spirit is the question you must face, moment by moment. And the ego does not give up easily.

The ego has a false pride and a need to keep its identity validated. It is impossible for it to experience the kind of qualities and behaviors that the inner spirit displays. But the ego is so clever that it will often pretend to have these qualities.

There are even courses on how to behave and act like a leader. Most of these courses are really methods that train the ego to be an even better actor.

Leadership is not changing your behavior by finding new ways to "act." It is an internal transformation that allows you to have the vision and clarity of a true leader.

Students of these courses are not expressing the spirit within—their true inner greatness. Because it is inauthentic, those interacting with those ego-driven leaders recognize it as a facade. Nor does pretending to be enlightened leaders bring about the synergism and combined creative energy that comes from igniting the spark of brilliance in others.

Authentic leaders know that they are not the identity that the role requires. Enlightened leaders operate from trust and faith in the universal energy and see everyone as equal, regardless of the role.

Jim is a general in the Air National Guard as well as a partner with a large law firm. He is a leader in both the military and the private sector. His experiences and understanding from working with hundreds of people has led to his qualities of what I call "enlightened leadership."

He intuitively knows that, regardless of rank in the military or status in private industry, people are all the same. He does not place himself above or below others and, in fact, recognizes everyone at all levels for the inner spirit.

Being a general comes with many external acknowledgments because of the hierarchy and deference to rank. For example, if he walks into a large room with hundreds of military men and women, they all stand. When he flies into a military base, he is greeted with salutes from everyone and a staff car is awaiting his arrival.

Jim says that there are a few officers who actually believe that these "required" accolades and military courtesies elevate them above the masses. These few believe their role as an officer defines their identity—an identity they consider superior to others.

They are "overcome by their own fumes" is a phrase he uses to describe the facade these individuals want to claim as their true identity.

In the private sector, Jim honors all others in his law firm on an equal basis. He does not allow office size, position, or gender to be reasons to see people as separate or inferior. He walks his talk and expects others in his firm to treat each other as equals.

Jim does not require personal fame or attention because he is connected to his inner authentic self. Anyone who knows Jim recognizes this wonderful quality in him. He is the kind of person people like to be around and because of his sincere approach to life and others, he is held in high esteem. He does not seek this recognition. He is a man who operates from integrity and always expresses himself with honesty.

Yet even Jim, with all his inner confidence and experience, has had those subtle thoughts from the ego slip into his dialogue.

"I wonder if I have one too many stars or stripes?" he has asked himself. "I wonder if I'm not operating several levels above my competency?"

If someone, operating at the level Jim is, can momentarily feel that inner doubt, it is easy to understand how the ego-driven leader, who has no inner power, must be operating from massive fear.

I asked Jim how it is that he doesn't get caught up in these two powerful roles that he plays on these two different stages? Jim thanks his wife for not allowing him to ever think any of those dramas change him from who he really is. For example, on one occasion she picked him up from the airport after he returned from one of his "dignitary" roles and reminded him that he forgot to take out the garbage.

I cannot stress too much the *intense dilemma* that occurs when you begin to challenge your ego.

Looking behind the ego's mask is a huge step and it demands surrender of the ego's need for the external. No one passes this test easily, and it is given to you over and over again in many different scenes and episodes. The question is to always put your *self* in the hot seat—not someone else.

Invoke your inner spirit to help you see what is the lesson for *you* in any situation that brings up the slightest anxiety or emotion. The ego will find this difficult because it automatically wants to blame another. Only as your confidence and trust in your inner authentic self grows stronger does this start to become easier.

DEMONSTRATION IN THE WORKPLACE

Practicing the new insights, as situations occur in the workplace, is essential. Your new understanding will not last if it is not demonstrated to one's self through right action. Much like a dream, which upon waking up is so clear but then slips into the unconscious mind and is lost, so is your new learning if not practiced with others.

Demonstrating to one's self and others is not easy. It is like a baby beginning to take his first steps. Picture the child, standing and tottering, falling and getting up again. He continues getting up, tottering, and falling. But the steps begin to get steadier, and the child grows in confidence. The child never gives up but delights in the progress as he steadily becomes proficient.

Insights that are not practiced or demonstrated are useless. Reading and studying, for the sake of accumulating wisdom, will only result in the person who talks a good story but doesn't "walk his talk."

Recognizing opportunities, when your ego is hooked, is the beginning. Take a moment to remind your self that there are better ways to respond. It is, at this moment, that you need to practice your new insight.

At first, it will be difficult to resist the ego's immediate desire to react. Bring yourself to the present situation and stop replaying the past. Feel the calmness you are able to bring to yourself. You are waking up from the unconscious desire to react and the unconscious dream that this is reality.

If the ego is still persistent, remind yourself that this is not about the other person. This is about you.

What is your perceived threat that causes you to want to react? Discovering the underlying cause for feeling the emotion you are experiencing is the key here.

Acknowledging the thought system that you created will release you. Repressing, denying, or rejecting the feelings keeps them under the surface and keeps you hostage to your ego. Identifying the source and then releasing it lead to freedom. Freedom from the constraints of the ego is what this book is about.

How does the ego and the inner spirit operate differently on a day-to-day basis? The following chart shows some examples of comparison:

EGO (operating from fear)	**SPIRIT** (operating from love)
Defending	Non-resistant and relaxed
Attempting to be superior	Accepting everyone as equal
Controlling outcomes and others	Trusting and detached
Gossiping	No need to put others down
Blaming and attacking	Looks within
Needing to be right	Can say I am wrong
Creating enemies	Extends love to everyone
Judging others	Sees everyone as equal
Unaccountable	Is willing to be the cause
Being a victim or martyr	Is responsible for self
Boasting	Has authentic power
Self-righteous	Compassion for others

Needing to have the first and the last say	Is calm and patient
Feeling obligated	Chooses freely
Feeling anxious or upset	Feels inner joy and contentment
Using addictions to stay numb	Has inner serenity
Complaining	Is trusting
Feeling unworthy	Has inner connection to the eternal source
Is inconsistent and conflicted	Has integrity
Denial of any of the above	Is open and free

I would also like to emphasize that your ego is not "bad." We simply give it too much power.

We need our ego to live in this world, but we must challenge it when it is running the show.

I compare the ego to a passenger in our car. We do not let it drive, but it is helpful on the journey. Sometimes it can sit right up in the front seat with us and at times it must ride in the back seat. I have even had times where it was necessary to lock my ego in the trunk.

My friend, Pat, who is working very diligently on her path of evolution, said there are times she would like to "kick her ego to the curb." But then, she realized that she would have no personality at all.

It is a fine line as you travel on your spiritual assignment. Be gentle with your ego as you would a little child. It is, after all, operating from the past when you were a little child.

But you do need to repeatedly challenge it and its belief system with the right questions. The questions, which will help you choose spirit over ego, always direct you back to yourself.

LEADERSHIP IS NOT FOR PERSONAL GAIN

Many employees tell me that those, who seek personal gain and see the employees as the method to bring that about, lead their organization. This is sometimes for financial gain or sometimes it is for personal glory.

True leaders do not see others as stepping-stones to their own personal empire or platform. A true leader has compassion and caring for everyone and understands the intrinsic rewards of operating from integrity.

T. J. Meenach was my grandfather. He was one of the finest men I ever knew and was a wonderful example of an enlightened leader. He served as president of the local park board and was a leader in the development of the park systems in our city. He worked tirelessly, and there are many beautiful projects for the enjoyment of generations to come, due to his efforts.

He was also a very successful realtor but never had need for personal recognition. He worked quietly behind the scenes in most things that he did. Because he didn't seek after lots of material acquisitions, he was very financially stable. When the depression hit, he was one of the few not threatened by it.

What he did do was to confidentially help many families who were struggling during that time. He loaned money and gave many people the lifeline they needed to survive. Even today, prominent people whom I meet tell me that their family business would not be here today were it not for my grandfather.

He worked toward the betterment of our community and taught strong values to his own children. My mother, the youngest of four, recalls the Christmas that she begged for a new red bicycle. All her friends had new bikes and their families were less prosperous.

Christmas morning arrived and there next to the tree stood her older brother's used bike, hand-painted red. It was not that he was not generous because he was. He came forth on many occasions to help his children, but he also taught them values and honest virtues.

He engaged in many worthy causes in our community and even became a state legislator for a period of time. He died when I was fifteen years old, but he left a memorable legacy for all of us. Although he never sought personal fame, after his death, a prominent bridge and street were named after him. I have had the gratification of working on some volunteer civic projects and feel he is smiling down at me for carrying on what he started.

GROUP WILL OR TEAMWORK

Group will is the powerful and dynamic force that is the result of alignment with each other toward a common purpose. This occurs when the leader is the conduit for energy and creativity that is flowing from the group.

Group will is the force that cuts through fear and obstacles to reach a common vision with the energy and creativity to accomplish it. It is so powerful that it attracts the right people, circumstances, and events needed to achieve the goal.

It is group will that draws others to the common purpose and realigns individuals to work together. This synchronicity and synergism seem almost magical, as if unseen forces are at work. Indeed, that is actually what is occurring.

Throughout history are many examples of leaders creating this synergism among thousands of people. It is this teamwork that companies often strive for but unfortunately, rarely achieve, except for platitudes and empty slogans.

An obvious characteristic of a group, who is truly practicing teamwork, is the lack of scrambling for personal gain and recognition. Individuals acknowledge each other for their contributions and accomplishments.

Open and trusting communication is essential in the group process and the leader can provide that atmosphere. Learning to recognize when others are in their "ego," especially if they are being defensive, is crucial to guiding a group. Not allowing their ego to hook yourself or others is a skill that comes from challenging your own ego.

How do you deal with someone individually or in the group who is using ego-defense mechanisms?

Asking the right questions of them to help understand and let go of their need to prevail is the best method. Talk to them in a voice of gentleness, as though they are little children because, at that moment, they are.

Your gentleness can bring down walls and help them stop feeling that they must defend or resist something. The emotion that they are experiencing is actually inside them and not really caused by the group. Seeing the spirit in others also requires not validating their ego when it shows up in the group.

One thing I have noticed in real teamwork is the word "we" being used in most situations. The frequent use of words such as "I" and "my" is usually a red flag that the egos are in reign instead of the spirit of the team—the "esprit de corps."

I have heard CEOs, who claim to be benevolent and team-oriented, use language like "my company," "my outlying property," "my" this or that. They are unaware that their language betrays their ego's need to build a personal empire. They don't understand that reaching a goal that benefits more than the self and personal agendas is what drives a real team effort. They are missing that deep inner satisfaction of true teamwork that elevates everyone.

I had an occasion to visit Chad Little and his race car team in Charlotte, North Carolina. I didn't know much about Nascar racing, but I always thought it was a one-person sport—the driver. I learned on this trip that was not the case at all.

Every person who was part of the team used the word "we" when referring to the actual race. "*We* won third place last week." "*We* are racing in Darlington next week." Whether you worked on the engine, changed the tires, or drove the race car, you were all a part of the team. Only the driver was famous, but nobody cared. They were all part of the team.

There are no prejudices in a group that is aligned to one common purpose. Everyone respects one another and understands that each person plays an essential role. The enlightened leader shines light on everyone equally and they respond in turn.

Janice is the owner of a very successful restaurant in the downtown business district of a city in the Pacific Northwest. She is in her mid-forties, although she looks much younger. She has owned a popular Italian restaurant for ten years. She had no formal education and had spent much of her early adult years as a waitress.

The mother of five children and a very energetic and loving spirit, she knew she wanted to do more than just work in a restaurant. She studied and became a licensed stockbroker, but that didn't fill her passion.

Janice always had a connection to her inner spirit. She calls it "the light." Ten years ago she heard about a restaurant that was not doing very well that was for sale. She offered them half of what they wanted and they took the offer. She somehow managed to gather the money, mostly on a wing and a prayer.

Today her wonderful little Italian restaurant and bar are always busy with people from the nearby businesses as well as from all over town. It isn't just because the food is good, although it is. And isn't just because the atmosphere is very cozy with overstuffed chairs, wicker furniture, and a variety of antique pieces, although it is that, too.

Going to Janice's restaurant *just feels good.* It seems to have its own personality. Whenever I mention going there to my associates, they always exclaim that they simply love it. It exudes warmth and old-world charm. People like to go there year round.

What is the secret to her success?

Janice said it has to do with "light." She believes that the restaurant is an entity—that it is a whole energy consciousness made up of the people who work there. And if anyone isn't feeling a part of the light—if they are in darkness, she gives them more light.

As the leader, she is responsible for sharing her light and helping them all be a part of it. They return it to her and each other, working as a team.

She compares it to all the employees being in the same boat. Why would you not want to do everything to make sure everyone in your boat is happy?

She believes each individual is integral to the success of the business. For example, the dishwasher is extremely important because without clean dishes the restaurant couldn't operate. Each person is part of a symphony: each with a different instrument but playing the same tune.

If on occasion, someone is so unhappy that the light from the group doesn't seem to help, then they might leave and that is okay too. She doesn't want darkness in her restaurant.

Janice's two sons work for her and do an excellent job. One time she had an employee who was complaining about her sons. This employee was about the same age as her sons. Rather than becoming defensive, she looked at this young man and said to herself, "I think he needs some mothering light. He wants to be a son."

She began shining extra light and attention on him; the complaints stopped. In addition, he started working harder because he felt more of a part in the "family" and had a greater commitment to the team. He became a shining example of what kindness and compassion can do for a person whose ego is feeling insecure or threatened.

Janice intuitively understands the energetic power of synergism and group will. Her restaurant continues to prosper and draws people for not only the delicious aroma of garlic and Italian cuisine, but also for the sense of friendliness and warmth that fills the restaurant. This comes from enlightened leadership and her genuine "light."

ENERGY AND LIGHT

An enlightened leader has a consciousness that is light and energetic.

Science tells us that we are each an energy system and that everything is energy. Our energy is a reflection of our consciousness.

As we grow in our path to our spiritual essence, our vibrational level becomes lighter. In addition, we feel lighter and more energetic. Synchronicity and spontaneity are natural to the enlightened leader because the enlightened leader's energy attracts others.

Control and drama cause you to experience a depletion of energy, and you will not be able to operate from the lightness that comes from trust and patience. The agonizing episodes of high drama are exhausting, and they actually cause you to feel heavy and burdened.

The authenticity of true leaders is recognized, and they are sought after. Enlightened leaders find the path of expression easy and effortless. People are drawn to them.

JoAnn never planned to be a leader, but it seemed to be her destiny. Her life just unfolded in that direction. She worked in a large bank and through her intelligence, integrity, and ability to make clear decisions, she rose through the ranks to the vice-president level. She was later persuaded to go to work for one of the largest companies in her city, where she also rose to the vice-presidential level.

JoAnn, at 5'3", has an angelic face, soft voice, and very kind demeanor. She is not the picture of the "power woman" one might expect. JoAnn never needed the pseudo-aggressive approach adopted by many women in an attempt to climb the corporate ladder. But then, JoAnn never attempted to rise up through the corporate structure. Her authentic power and ability to contribute to the success of an organization were recognized, however.

One of her former bosses told me that JoAnn was one of the finest people he had ever known. He also said to make no mistake about her power, despite her petite stature and gentle acumen. He described her as having an ability to have great insights into things he hadn't even considered and for which he was very grateful.

They had a great team at this company, and they interacted freely in the workplace. She walked into his office any time she wanted to talk to him. However, he knew something serious was on her mind when she made an actual appointment with him. That was a signal for him that he better be prepared because she always spoke with very clear intention.

Even if he resisted at first, her ideas or suggestions always ended up being absolutely right, causing him to see something he had not thought of. He was very indebted for her recognition of possible obstacles or situations that hadn't occurred to him.

He recalls she was also more than able to deal with some of the egos in the workplace. One particular person was causing a big "drama" and trying to exert his pressure and influence on others in a way to fit his personal agenda. He had issued a memo earlier in the day to all the employees that JoAnn felt was extremely unfair.

The president watched her unobtrusively walk over to the man's office door, go in, and close the door behind her. He heard a loud exchange of voices—not yelling but a very vehement conversation. Then she quietly emerged and went back to work as though nothing happened. This was not unusual for JoAnn.

The man then came out of his office a little bit later, slightly red-faced and proceeded to send out another memo, changing the ego-motivated original one. He came to a meeting later that day with an entirely different attitude. JoAnn knew how to speak her mind for the betterment of the organization, and she didn't back down.

Another person who worked with JoAnn as an officer in the company told me that she impacted his life in a positive way. JoAnn told him that he was discriminating against her as a female by not listening to her and discounting her in meetings. He was taken aback at first but after trying to deny it, began to slowly recognize that she was telling him the truth.

She was the first woman with the courage to challenge his behavior and, though he resisted it at first, her words challenged him to change. He now holds her in great esteem and after that confrontation, she became his best confidante and trusted associate.

JoAnn became chair of the board of the local Chamber of Commerce, only the second woman in the history of the Chamber to be elected to that position. In her many activities with diverse groups, she has a natural gift for helping people move into alignment toward a higher principle.

She has an ability to step back, listen to everyone, and see the bigger picture. From that vantage point, she can lead others to move to a higher lever. She doesn't hesitate to ask people directly to put aside their personal agendas and seek an answer for the common good of the group. She knows how to ask the right questions to help bring clarity to the group and facilitate open communication.

How did JoAnn learn and develop all these leadership qualities?

I recall her acceptance speech for her chair of the Chamber, given to 1,200 business and community leaders. She was describing the "education and training" that had prepared her for her career in business and civic affairs.

JoAnn had grown up in a family with five sisters and two brothers. She was the middle child. They were reared by her mother who was an incredible woman and who taught her three rules:

- ◆ DON'T WHINE
- ◆ DON'T FIGHT
- ◆ ALWAYS TELL THE TRUTH

JoAnn said she also recalled her mother telling them, "Many hands make light work."

These simple edicts from a hard-working and loving mother were profound lessons in living life authentically. These simple words are also the foundation of teamwork and honoring one another: a goal to which businesses and organizations everywhere are aspiring but rarely attaining.

JoAnn is admired and liked by so many people. She never sought personal glory or fame, but she has attained it in her community and region. She has earned the respect of both men and women for her sincere and dedicated leadership. I am honored that she is my friend.

Throughout history we have many examples of great leaders. They have been studied and emulated, analyzed and worshipped.

RODNEY EDWARD GANNON

I would like to put on center stage someone who demonstrated the qualities of enlightened leadership that deeply impacted my life: Rodney Edward Gannon. Mr. Gannon, to those who worked for him, was an amazing man.

I was thirty-five years old when I went to work for a large radiology practice in my city. They had four offices, a radiology practice in the hospital, and they traveled to several outlying regions. I was hired as their marketing director.

I had seven doctors whom I worked for, but I worked most directly for Mr. Gannon, the business manager. I didn't know at the time that he would forever change my life. I didn't know that he would continue to be a source of inspiration and an example of what is so needed in the workplace today.

Mr. Gannon was a red-haired Catholic Irishman with twelve children. He was not a big man, maybe 5'9" or 5'10", with a bad back. He often stood up during meetings and leaned against the wall while talking or listening.

He was the most direct man in all his conversations and, yet, he never seemed to intimidate or offend anyone. He was a straight shooter—take it or leave it. I often watched other men size him up and look like they were ready to take him on. But Mr. Gannon's genuine "hold back nothing" approach always disarmed them.

When in any kind of negotiations, he would just speak frankly and put everything on the table. He would lean back in his chair and never seemed in a hurry or anxious at all. He had no strategy except to find a solution or agreement that would truly become a winning situation for both parties. He always seemed to ask them just the right question.

Coming from a sales and marketing background, I thought you always had a strategy. I noticed how others always kept one "ace in the hole" so that they could triumph in the interaction. Not Mr. Gannon. And if things would start to get even slightly heated by the other party, he would lean back in his chair and chuckle in an understanding way, which would help them put down their defenses and come to a resolution.

One of the greatest things that Mr. Gannon did for me was to give me his full confidence. He told me to go out and do grand things. He told me I was remarkable and capable, and that he wanted me to excel. He said that no matter what happened, he would always support me, even if I made a mistake.

"But if you make the same mistake twice," he said, "we'd probably have to talk about that." Still, I would learn from it.

Can you how imagine how well I worked under him?

He was truly the wind beneath my wings.

I excelled and achieved more than I ever thought possible. It was a wonderful time while I grew in my own authentic power and inner confidence under his special guidance. I had no fear, and he fanned my spark of creativity. If leaders and managers would all do that for those they lead, they would be amazed at the power and potential in others, just waiting to be ignited.

Mr. Gannon was like a warm-hearted wise uncle to me, besides being a great business manager. He would often come and get me, so we could take a walk outside and talk about the business. He would share strategies and ideas for the future, and ask my opinion. I felt valued and included in the direction of the company, which gave me a real sense of contributing in a meaningful way.

One day, as we were waiting for a board meeting to get started, I naively mentioned a bill for an x-ray I recently had. I received the bill from our own company and the bill had a mistake on it.

"Let me see that," Mr. Gannon said.

He looked perplexed and the doctors laughed that the bill had such a blatant error on it, especially since I was an actual employee. I thought nothing more about it.

What I didn't know at the time was that this same error had gone out to over 10,000 patients. It happened because we were in a computer conversion and it turned out to be a big problem that took a lot of sorting out and much time wasted.

Mr. Gannon called me in to his office right after the meeting and asked me why I would do such a thing. I had brought up a mistake that he was responsible for to the doctors and the mistake made him look stupid.

"Why didn't you just come to me?" he asked. "I would never have done something like that to you in front of the doctors."

I was devastated. I had been so ignorant and flippant about this "funny little error," not even thinking about how it affected him. I had been thoughtless, and it was at his expense—at the expense of the man I thought walked on water.

I apologized profusely begging for forgiveness. He just looked steadily at me and then quietly asked me to leave.

For the first time, at any time, in my career, I felt like breaking down and crying. I went to my office and closed the door. I tried to work, but I felt numb.

I kept reliving it over and over, wondering what I could do to fix things. I thought of sending flowers, writing him a long letter, going back down to his office and saying I was sorry again.

Suddenly, I had a huge shift in my own thinking. I became aware that I was not thinking so much about him—I was worried about me. I felt like I had fallen from grace, and I wanted to do something to elevate myself in his eyes once again. I wanted his benevolent light to shine on me again. I wasn't really thinking about him at all.

This was a startling thought. To put it in the language of this book, I was "looking behind the face of my ego." I didn't like what I saw. (We rarely do like to see our ego's schemes for saving face.)

I grew up that day. I learned I didn't have to be the "little darling" that I liked to see myself as. I needed to be authentic and responsible for my actions. I intuitively knew that I needed to let him be.

I quietly worked in my office, feeling the pain but knowing I would grow through this, too. Then I heard a knock at my door. It was Mr. Gannon.

"Danna, let's take a walk."

He had a serious look on his face, but I was ready to face this conversation. I was remorseful, but also fully accountable for my lack of professionalism.

For once in my life, I shut up. I just let him talk. What he said endeared me to him more than words can describe.

"Danna, please forgive me."

He asked me to *forgive him*! He said his reaction was just coming from his pride and his desire to always have a perfect business office and a smooth running organization. He realized my intention was not to embarrass him and was sorry that he had gotten upset with me.

Now I could hardly hold the tears back. This great man was asking me to forgive him for what I had caused.

That was the first time when I understood a truly enlightened leader is one who does not operate from a false pride or ego that needs to be superior. This wise man could say he was wrong, even though what I did was good cause for his reaction.

I have never forgotten that lesson. It was the kind that moves you deeply inside. It was like I had been digging with a shovel to move some land and then a fault in the earth just moved the land effortlessly in one felt swoop. The shift in my consciousness and understanding was that immense.

Mr. Gannon died a year ago. His twelve children and wife had the benefit of his loving guidance as a wonderful husband and father. I had his presence for three incredible years. He will remain forever in my heart as someone who encouraged me not only in my own growth, but unknowing to him, he also inspired in me the passion to write this book and teach my seminars. I think he is smiling down now, too.

INNER SATISFACTION

Leading others from an open and trusting heart is so necessary in these turbulent times.

Giving positive appreciation and recognition are not bad ways to help motivate others. And it is certainly far better than intimidating them. But there is something even deeper for an individual that inspires them to higher levels of expression.

It comes from the internal satisfaction of knowing you are making a difference. It is the inner awareness that you are contributing to the betterment of the world in some way that is meaningful to you. This kind of fulfillment cannot be given to someone or handed out from another person. It is intrinsic.

My dear friend, Angelo, a brilliant radiologist, calls this "psychic income." We all strive for financial income, but the real fulfillment is the inner knowledge that you are helping someone else and that you are giving from your full potential.

A radiologist is the doctor's doctor. The primary care physician deals with the patients directly, and the radiologist usually doesn't even see the patients. Yet his ability to read the images from CAT Scans, MRIs, etc., is critical to diagnosing the patient's disease or injury.

That is all the radiologist needs: the internal satisfaction.

The primary physician receives the thanks and appreciation, but the radiologist knows he helped that person without any outward recognition for it. He knows his talent and dedication is improving the health for many people, even if he never sees them. That is "psychic" income.

That inner essence of expression through working with your passion cannot be given—only experienced. Motivation by fear or motivation by incentives is relying on something external to incite action. It will be a temporary motivation at best.

The deep satisfaction of enriching the lives of others can only be felt within. As an enlightened leader, you can provide that opportunity for those you lead by creating an environment where people can contribute from their inner spirit.

Seeing the genius in others by recognizing the spirit in them is the highest level of leadership. Indeed, it is the only leadership.

CHAPTER TEN

The Final Performance

INTEGRATION AND BECOMING WHOLE

How can you be an enlightened leader that leads others to higher levels of achievement, potential, and success if you are not whole and complete?

This chapter is about the integration of your ego self with your higher self, so that you can operate from that enlightened space of leadership that fans the spark of passion, creativity, and joy in the workplace.

This book and its teachings are consistent with ancient wisdom and philosophies, applied anew. What I am describing to you is how these universal truths that have stood the test of time still pertain to your workplace today. They are as relevant to today's workplace environment of individuals in pain, as they were in earliest times with previous generations.

Biblical stories, ancient philosophies, Greek and Roman mythology, Eastern religions and teachings, and historical passages of great leaders—all contain the truths and wisdom that have been a source of learning for people seeking answers and purpose.

Through the centuries, there have been many changes in people and how we live. We work differently. We look and dress differently. We travel and even talk differently. Technology through the ages has dramatically changed the world. Even the physical environment of our planet has gone through huge transitions.

Yet human beings are not different.

Man's search for meaning and purpose has been consistent throughout time. Human beings' need for love, families, social structure, and interaction has endured. Wars, famine, suffering, and pain have also continued through the ages. Now, here we are today, in our advanced and sophisticated world of high technology and ever-evolving modern creations.

And *we are still suffering.*

We try to deny the dissatisfaction and lack of meaning with the attainment of external stimuli and validation, keeping us blind to the suffering. When our own plate is full, it does make it easier not to think about the starving of others' souls.

But we cannot keep discontent hidden all the time. One place it is showing up most intensely is the workplace. The workplace is a huge stage where millions of people interact every day. A new understanding and compassion in the world and the workplace are needed.

Now is the time for leaders to begin the process of changing the environment worldwide. The time has come to elevate understanding and to bring clarity to the masses. This change now will create a better world for future generations.

IDENTIFYING THE SOURCE OF FEAR

So where do we begin?

The way out of this massive dream of pain and suffering finally occurs when momentary pleasures and occasional glimpses of joy are no longer enough to keep the pain from surfacing. This gives us the chance to look at the fears below the surface. The former tactics for blocking awareness then begin to be exposed. The strategies to keep doubt and fear hidden can start to be recognized and given up.

Leaders and managers who go through this process can be a shining example, as well as a conduit to those being led, to release their own great fears and barriers so they might also reach their true potential of creativity, joy, and peacefulness.

But they have to become aware that they are operating from fear.

Identifying your fears and the need to defend or deny them are primary to your evolution. Bringing them to the surface by not suppressing feelings is the only way this will happen. Awakening occurs as we allow walls and old patterns to surface in our interactions.

Re-experiencing the same issues is the only way to see the patterns of our past that are keeping us stuck in replaying it today. It is essential to face the pain from the past. When we can do that, it leads to letting go of predictable ways that we have established to validate or protect ourselves.

When you don't know the cause of the pain or the issue creating it, remembrance or the ability to "re-experience" has the purpose of revealing it to you. The intent of remembering is to heal old wounds of the past, so you can move forward.

Clearing the static, caused by the energy expended in the protective mechanisms, will allow you to connect to your true source, your inner guidance.

Through facing hidden pain, you can distinguish the mold your ego has developed to keep it concealed. Recognizing the ancient pain is like cracking a hardened shell of protection. This breakthrough will give you a whole new perspective, leading to freedom and peace within yourself.

Understanding the theater concept and your role in acting out your hidden motives and plot assists you to see more clearly, with fewer defenses. Keeping in mind that you cast all others in your drama helps you distinguish their reactions from your own. It gives you the opportunity for ownership of your feelings and the chance to look inside. But it takes committed attention to do this.

Learning to notice when you are feeling any kind of anxiety or negative feelings is so important.

Observing yourself when you project any of your negative feelings on others can be an opening for you. It can reveal to you the hidden pain. Your ego wants to deny that there is any pain, but your soul is asking you to pay attention so you can let the feelings emerge.

In our culture, identifying the fear or pain, is usually more difficult for men because of the conditioning that says men don't feel pain. Men want to appear strong, but this is still the ego trying to appear fearless.

If you are wondering if you are denying any pain or resisting any demons beneath the surface, just notice if you get angry, controlling, defensive or rely on addictions to reduce anxiety.

Notice if you blame the government, your spouse, the other drivers on the road, your co-workers, or anyone else for your anxiety, anger, pain, or guilt. If you do, your ego is trying to expel pain.

UNDERSTANDING EMOTIONS

The current problems with road rage, racial riots, sports rage among the parents of children in soccer, baseball, etc., the battles in the workplace, and the conflicts in government are all examples of misplaced anger. Misdirected anger is pain within yourself that is surfacing and being expressed outwardly.

This misplaced emotion is also due to the powerlessness and insecurity that people are feeling today.

However, denied emotions do surface, and this aggression is often uncontrollable when it does finally come out. Suppressed feelings cause an even greater intensity of emotion.

Repressing feelings is a sure way to create over-exaggerated emotions, interactions, and reactions. Many crimes are the result of unexpressed feelings finally coming forth in an uncontainable way.

The expression of emotions is essential to the well being of humans. Denying emotions and trying to hide your fears are the cause of conflicts everywhere. So understanding emotions is essential here.

Feeling emotion is the ability that spirit has given to humans so that we can fully experience and appreciate the physical world. The many ranges of emotions provide us a variety of experiences depending on what is occurring in our world.

Pleasure, for example, is derived, when your desires are being met. Sadness occurs during circumstances that are difficult, or it can be the result of a loss. Anger, which is actually fear being expressed aggressively, occurs when there is a perceived threat.

Pure love is not an emotion. Pure love is the essence, the light, and the energy of the universe.

But love is clouded by your judgment and the constrictions of your ego.

The experience of love in the physical world is an emotion. It can be experienced as compassion, empathy, joy, sentiment, understanding, friendship, romance, affinity, and familial love, to name a few. Love is expressed through words, actions, attitudes, and commitment. It is also expressed with physical touch. A human infant, for example, will not survive without physical touching and holding.

The elderly need and respond to physical touch, and often are those who receive the least. Working with the retirement industry, I watched the elderly happily receive the physical touch of family, caregivers, and even pets that were allowed to visit. They were energized and gratified by touch.

Emotion, when expressed fully, allows an exchange and free flow of energy that is not only good for the soul, but necessary. Laughing, crying, dancing, singing, writing, art, communication, and other expressions are experiences of emotions being released in a healthy and satisfying manner. Even expressing anger though aggression is healthy as long as it is not aimed at someone or causing someone harm.

Dreams also allow relief to the psyche from stress of unresolved issues of the day. They provide a free-flowing energy that is blocked during the waking state. Dreams also offer a glimpse into the wellspring of creativity that can be applied to your day in the waking reality.

Inspiration and understanding can occur in dreams. That is why it is helpful to remember and record them. They can contain keys to solving problems in all areas of your life. They are gentle reminders of the issues in your life that need to be addressed.

Many geniuses describe receiving their inspiration in a dream state.

The universe has a natural rhythm that is soothing to our soul. Watching the waves, rocking our babies, and dancing with our lovers are expressions of that rhythm. Drumming, enjoying music, chanting, and even pacing are expressions of the waves of movement that release emotions and balance our inner being.

I believe that soldiers marching in formation to a compelling rhythm can incite energy and emotion to go to battle. Marching together is also an expression of unity. Look at those who march in a parade, for example.

But even more importantly, I believe that swinging your arms and marching deliberately soothe the soul by expressing inner angst. The more intense the pain within, the greater is the need to express this rhythm. Look at the way Hitler's armies marched.

Suppressing emotions results in blocked energy. This blocked energy can be felt physically as stress, anxiety, stomachaches and headaches, general uneasiness, irritability, crankiness, tiredness, and moodiness. Unexpressed emotions eventually cause sickness, cancer, heart attacks, and other life-threatening diseases.

When you suppress your emotions, instead of allowing them to flow and be expressed, you are doing great damage to yourself. Denial is the tool by which the ego represses fear and pain to protect itself and to keep it below the surface where it does not have to be acknowledged.

Denial by your ego is so powerful that you do not even know you are doing it. You are missing the vital link to your freedom from this denial process.

Your ego is closing a door to your soul.

Defense and resistance are techniques your ego is using because we have learned it is not okay to have emotions. We are ashamed and afraid to appear weak so we hide our feelings from others, but most tragically, we hide them from ourselves.

Recognizing and experiencing emotions are key to understanding the issues needing attention so that you can advance from the ego state to the enlightened state.

The pain is deeply imbedded in your inner psyche from experiences of long ago. The pain will not stop being replayed until it is extricated. You will re-enact the scenes from the past because that is the your ego's script.

There is a secret, central belief beneath the surface that is self-deprecating, which the ego considers unacceptable. But looking at it will bring forth the very origin of the belief, and you will be set free as you allow light to shine on it.

The question to ask yourself, once again, is: "What am I afraid of?"

Only weakness and fear need defending. Remembering the origination of the event that you still have kept buried in your inner psyche is your release. And that release can only occur when you stop resisting, when you stop fighting or fleeing.

But getting to the origin of the fear is a challenge. It is always made difficult by the ego that does not want its release. The ego will project any suppressed feelings outward to avoid looking within. This occurs most dramatically in the workplace.

When inner, denied fears are projected outward, they become the formation of the "enemy" which is so central to the drama in the workplace, as well as the drama in the world.

If you allow it to come up and you look at it, you will see how it has been running your life. It was a decision you made as a child over some experience that you were hurt or shamed by.

Looking behind the face of the ego takes the most courage of your entire life. If it were easy, you would have done it long ago.

But it is really nothing now. It is in the past and it is over. But until you see it and tell it farewell, it will continue to cause your suffering.

Jerry was the head of a huge company with a salary and bonus system that gave him an annual income that neared a million dollars. He had everything money could buy, and power and status to go with it. But because he had not healed his soul, it was not enough.

Here, we see the example of the insatiable ego: All the external validations and material attainments did not remove the inner-core fear of rejection.

Jerry wielded huge power in the workplace, but could experience rejection if the grocery clerk was unfriendly. Not that he told anyone that, of course, because the ego denies everything.

Jerry's ego was a great actor—an Academy Award-winning actor, in fact. He knew how to appear benevolent when necessary, jovial when that was called for, and stern and intimidating when he needed that role. His success in creating great deals and moving the company forward had taken him to the top.

Then Jerry had a heart attack. It was a serious one, and it got his attention. Lying in the hospital, Jerry began to take stock of his life. He had everything he thought he would need to be happy and more. Yet he was burdened with stress and anxiety. It all seemed so meaningless in the face of his mortality.

His family had rushed to his bedside. For the first time, he saw and felt the significance of the people who loved him. He had been so busy pursuing the American dream that he had not valued the most meaningful parts of his life and the people who mattered. Where had the years gone?

Jerry, while quietly alone, realized his inner fears of rejection, and inadequacy had driven him to the height of success. It wasn't creative inspiration, but fear of failure, that led him to where he was today.

He had stepped on lots of toes to get there and had made enemies along the way. The power struggles in the company had caused a lot of dissension and pain for people in the workplace. He had projected his fears and pains onto the "enemies" and justified his actions.

He began to think about all the things he had missed in his life. He was now suddenly very grateful that his family had stayed with him through these turbulent years. He didn't deserve this much love.

Looking back, he saw the fear that originated when he was a child, and how it grew and directed his life on the stage at work. His fear and inadequacy could not be hidden from himself, despite all the external attainments of the ego.

Jerry started to listen to his inner guidance from the eternal source. He recognized how his endless need for validation had been driving him. He felt sadness for the people he had hurt along the way and realized they were not the enemies.

As he began forgiving his enemies, he also began forgiving himself. He finally saw that it was himself—his tiny but tenacious ego that was his only enemy. It took a heart attack to finally get his attention.

For some, even a heart attack does not get their attention.

The drama in the workplace is the source of the pain and misery we find occurring in all industries. The key to stopping the drama is to look within ourselves as unpleasant emotions occur. Every conflict, every subtle fear, or every angry outburst is an opportunity to learn about your self and ultimately, participate in ending the tragic drama in the workplace.

As a leader, your intention needs to be to end the fear in the workplace environment, thus allowing the freedom of expression of the many valuable people in the organization. But ending that fear must start with healing yourself by looking at what your emotions are telling you. Your emotions are the messengers of your heart and soul, helping you discover your true greatness that is lying beneath your self-created role.

Healing this worldwide epidemic of pain is the goal of this book. Nourishing our souls and bringing peace and understanding to the work environment are good places to begin. It is the intent of this book to help you utilize this information and restore you to your true identity, which is the real, whole, and complete self. As leaders, when you do that, you can also help others do the same.

RELIANCE

In the world of the ego, reliance is found with other people and things. Reliance is the act of counting on something or someone outside the self for some perceived needed support, validation, or assistance. But relying on things outside your self will never provide security.

The only reliance that will ever give you any kind of certainty is from your inner guidance.

Communion with spirit by connecting with your inner self will lead to genuine freedom, peace, and joy. Therein lies your safety and security, because this source is constant and unchanging. It can never be reduced or taken away, except by your own choice.

FEAR OF SACRIFICE

Your ego is afraid of losing something that it believes it needs to survive.

Accumulation of things and people that are evidence of its power and strength has been what the ego has been doing since its birth. These pieces of evidence that prove that the ego is worthy are held tightly and not given up easily.

These props on your stage are not necessary, but your ego clings desperately to them.

The one thing that will become apparent, as you begin to wake up, is that all these attempts to have and possess people and things will never provide the inner security that you are looking for. They are external evidence to show the world that the ego is worthy; they will not satisfy the soul.

Inanimate objects actually have no intrinsic value, but they do have an assigned value by your ego that desires them. For example, a luxury car and a castle-like home can be powerful forces for the ego that believes these accruements elevate its status to "king-like."

On the contrary, a small modest car and home can be symbols of righteousness and evidence that you are a humble and good person to another ego. Neither has any meaning at all, except what is assigned by the individuals who desire or create them in their lives.

People can even be a status symbol, seen as an accessory to bolster the ego and its appearance in society. It takes agreement on the part of both people for this to occur. An example is the selection of a partner of the opposite sex who has the appearance that enhances the ego of the other partner, i.e. the young and beautiful with a rich, older person.

When you prey on others by using them for external validation, it is ultimately unsatisfying for both parties, even if they unconsciously agree to it for awhile.

Parents often use their children to elevate their status by expecting them to perform and increase the parents' self-worth.

Group consciousness also affects the value of things within a group of people, such as different cultures, genders, ethnic groups, economic groups, etc. Diverse groups can hold the same objects and acquirements in entirely different lights and viewpoints.

Attachment to certain objects that identify a person to a special group is another example of reliance on the external for confirmation. If you feel a strong attachment to an object, then it is the ego using things outside itself to give you a sense of self-worth. Examples are as varied as logo clothes, fashions in clothing, as well as counter-culture garb, a favorite sports team memorabilia, uniforms, etc.

There is nothing wrong with these items. It is the attachment to people and things to elevate yourself and to give the ego an identity that creates the problem.

The ego fears losing them or sacrificing these false witnesses. The ego's attempt to keep you in this insane and ever-aspiring need for external objects is very seductive.

As you begin to wake up, this ludicrousness of believing an object or even attachment to another person is who you are, will begin to be realized. As you see that having things for the mere pleasure of enjoying them is one thing. Needing to attain them for your identity is absurd. The desperate grip of trying to keep these props in place will diminish. A new freedom will begin to be experienced.

The fear of sacrifice will be replaced with the inner peace of relying on your spiritual guidance.

Relying on the spirit within is the only way of experiencing trust. Trust brings such incredible peace of mind that it is wondrous that one would ever give it up. However, the ego wants to be in charge and wants to be right.

The fact that you continue to follow the familiar path of the ego is demonstrated whenever you have lack of trust in spirit and the universal process. When you truly trust in spirit, you need do nothing. You are secure. You can relax. This is intolerable to the ego; for the ego requires the drama.

In fact, the ego feeds off the drama for its sustenance.

Like children lost in a storm, individuals in every arena have fought their fear by the creation of the ego, which is an utterly hopeless attempt to be complete and happy. Instead, they have found themselves in the horrifying world of fear and doubt. And where they would seek joy, they discover empty, meaningless results with only some momentary pleasures, leaving them always seeking more.

The world is spinning out of control as is exemplified in the battles on all fronts, children having children, worldwide suffering, wars between countries, people killing each other and themselves, and the desperation in the souls of so many humans in all different places. This confusion and fear that is experienced as resignation, pain, and despair are all the results of people being disconnected from their true and eternal source.

The restoration of true peace and joy will come only from the reliance on spirit and the powerful inner self, rather than the tiny, helpless self-created ego.

The ego is temporary and will pass away. You spirit is eternal.

As the world learns reliance on spirit, it will bring about the transformation of the world.

While you are living in the physical world, there are only four things that won't change: truth, choice, time, and death. So while you are here, why not use your time wisely and choose the unchanging, eternal truth before you reach the point of death?

Choice is the function and the main component of free will. Choice is not always elected by the conscious mind. Since some of the decisions that are made come from your subconscious motives, you will need commitment and courage to bring them to the surface or to light.

Choice without purpose is the source of many individuals' chaotic life. Choice without spiritual intent can lead to destruction. However, choosing again is always an option within the time you are alive. But the consequences get more severe, the longer you delay your alignment with spirit and make choices with the ego.

The challenge is to give up being the victim, give up blaming, give up the envy and fear, and place your trust in spirit. That takes trust and perseverance. But when you do, the freedom is endless. You no longer need to defend. You no longer need to control outcomes. You no longer need to judge anyone or anything.

FORGIVENESS

Why is forgiveness so important?

As long as we judge others, we will continue to see the world and its people as separate from us. When we can learn that everyone else is simply playing out their script and they do not owe us a part in our drama, we can forgive.

As we see their path is perfect for them and it is what they need for their inner spirit to learn, we can forgive them. They aren't really doing anything to us.

As long as we see them as someone to play out our assigned role for them, we will judge their performance and hold them as wrong. We cannot forgive someone who we believe is doing something wrong to us.

Forgiveness brings our relief from pain.

It takes a great deal of intense emotion to keep holding someone wrong and responsible for our feelings. When we can see others as the same and no longer judge them, no matter what they are doing, we free up energy for ourselves.

When we can forgive ourselves, we will find peace. It is important to see and release what we find unacceptable and unforgivable in ourselves. But we can't forgive ourselves if we can't forgive others and we can't forgive others if we can't forgive ourselves.

When we forgive others and ourselves, we can find peace and joy.

Peace comes the moment we stop putting up barriers to it. In the past, there has been little peace. But we can move into the future to a place where love prevails and compassion is the order of the day.

And we can share that with our children. Then, they can share that with theirs. Children who are given choices in a loving, disciplined way, as they make the passage into adulthood, will usher in a new future for all the coming generations.

Joy is our natural inheritance. It is not learned. It cannot be sought after. It emerges when you lift the veil of illusion. The veil of illusion was created by the ego that says, "I am not worthy."

The ego seeks substitutes for joy outside itself. The attempts are temporary distractions that lead only to needing more from outside the self, rather than the source of joy, which is within. It is like drinking sweet beverages to satisfy your thirst . . . only to become thirstier.

WHAT WILL IT TAKE TO WAKE YOU UP?

It is time to put the spotlight on the entanglement of egos in the workplace, so the drama can be revealed and individuals can stop being hooked by their egos.

This web of reacting egos is the source of the ever-increasing situation of envy, pain, insecurity, and competition.

What does it take to wake you up and convince you that the ego's path is one of self-destruction? How much pain and suffering does it take for you to say there must be a better way?

You are caught in a trap. This much pain is not necessary.

Your ego's desire to keep you asleep is the cause of your pain. The ego is bound in time and space, and therefore, wants you to believe in the external rewards. It will win at all costs.

The ego's perseverance in needing to be right prevents you from looking clearly at what is really occurring in the workplace, as well as what's in your life.

When you find yourself trying to control anything or anyone, including yourself, know that it is the ego trying to prevail, to save face, or to keep you asleep.

Even trying to control your self is the ego because only the ego utilizes control.

The ego would like to place all consequences in your life as caused by someone or something outside yourself. This is not true. Your life is a reflection of the choices that only you have made—nothing more, nothing less.

The workplace is a mirror in which you have many opportunities to see how your ego is operating. You are always free to choose: ego or spirit?

Honoring others and seeing them as yourself is essential. What is within you is also within them.

As a leader, acknowledging their spirit and authentic power, in both your thoughts and your actions, frees others to contribute fully to the betterment of the organization. When leaders operate from the ego, they limit the true power and any possibility for contribution by all members of the team.

Judging or in any way demeaning others hurts not only them, but actually harms you more by limiting your ability to see clearly. Unhooking from the ego requires giving up judgment, comparison, envy, and even pity.

Seeing someone as incapable or not as able as you is still your judgment that you are superior. Seeing others as separate, as different, inferior, or superior is simply your ego placing values on others. What you see is not true.

In an organization, all the people have contributions to make when they are not limited by the assessment or need to be superior by the egos in leadership positions.

As a leader, you must adamantly do away with any feelings of conquering, triumphing, or in any way setting yourself above those being led. Causing people to be submissive, based on the corporate structure or the organizational system, which places people above and below one another, is so destructive to those being led.

The voice of your inner spirit is trying to talk to you at all times. How often do you heed it?

Spirit will use any experience or situation to talk to you, if you will allow it, and gently speaks to you in many ways: through music, seeming coincidences, words or comments from others, books, movies, relationships and interactions, and finally, if you don't listen—through pain and suffering.

If you aren't hearing your inner guidance, it is because you are not paying attention.

Perhaps your ego is speaking so loudly that there is no room for another voice. Your soul is persistent, though, because your full integration and restoration to your inner greatness is your destiny. It is why you are here. It is your true purpose.

THE AUTHENTIC HIGHER SELF

Let's look at the ways the authentic, higher self lives and operates.

The true self knows it is love and part of the source of the ultimate creativity and intelligence. Therefore, the real self does not need to feel superior. It sees others as equal and not separate.

The real self is trusting in a greater plan and lives in the present, allowing events to unfold naturally, rather than trying to control outcomes for itself and others. Because it trusts, it understands that all events have a purpose and an opportunity for learning. There is no need to judge any circumstances or others.

The authentic self accepts what is. It doesn't have to fix others. It asks for nothing and receives everything.

The real self is, therefore, patient and understanding. It knows all things happen in their own time. And because of the respect the real self holds for others, others are drawn to this self in response to the genuine sense of acceptance.

The higher self operates from inspiration and wisdom, its true source of creativity and intelligence, so it is deeply satisfied expressing its abundance of natural abilities and talents.

The true self is consistent at all times because it is not in a self-created role that changes with the drama occurring. Others feel this integrity, which results in trust from those in the workplace.

The authentic, higher self is a good leader because the powerful qualities of a leader are a natural result of giving up the ego's artificial needs. The true self is connected to its source and reliant on that center of tranquility in all situations.

And finally, the higher self is not afraid because it knows its natural inheritance is joy, peace, and love.

By being present to those qualities while living life fully, the higher self experiences all situations as natural and part of its physical life path, an opportunity to share and extend love to others.

The higher self does not hold others responsible for happiness and forgives others for what they "didn't" do.

The higher self is free. The higher self is at peace.

You have a choice: (1) to operate in the frenzied manner of the ego or (2) to operate in the powerful and peaceful state of the higher self who is not disconnected from its source.

When something occurs that causes your ego to react, if you can see the futileness of its battle, even if only for a moment, you can begin to release the death grip of the ego.

That is why *The Course in Miracles* says, "Who would attempt to fly with the tiny wings of the sparrow when the mighty wings of an eagle have been given him?"

Ask yourself the following questions when you are feeling anxiety or any reaction of negativity:

- Am I judging this person as inferior or superior to me?
- Do I think I know what this person should do or say?
- Am I trying to control the outcome of this situation?
- When I feel anxiety or stress what do I do? Do I throw myself into an addiction? What is the addiction(s)?
- Do I avoid feeling my emotions? Can I express them in a healthy way?
- Do I attempt to numb myself with addictive behavior?
- Do I have any stress-related illnesses? What pain or fear am I blocking?
- Am I present or am I reacting from the past or worrying about the future?
- When do I feel guilty? Is it true?
- What are the props in life (the external objects to validate myself)? How attached to them am I? What would I hate to sacrifice?

As you become more connected to your inner spirit, you will be restored to your authentic self.

This is what integration is: removing the blocks, clearing away the clouds of judgment, and allowing your inner spirit to emerge.

CHOOSE THE PATH OF INTEGRATION

What should you do with this information? How should you apply this information?

Become more powerful. Recognize a better way to interact with others while on the earth. Pay attention to the opportunities to see the ego reflected back to your self. Gravitate toward Truth by reading books, attending seminars, meditating, and all other methods for awakening. Stay focused with the intent to wake up.

Absolute freedom is the goal. Short term is the relief from pain and misery.

Choose well when you see opportunities for advancement. Welcome options that lead to a new direction and to new possibilities. Stop feeding off addictions that cause you to remain unconscious.

Your very power is being denied with every choice you make to side with the ego. Take not this lightly.

Demonstrate your affinity toward others, your compassion for the suffering, and your faith in spirit. Do not seek after personal glory and attention, as it will become a stumbling block to your awakening.

Choose wisely. Stop self-suffering by identifying the thought system that is pulling you down and then, choose differently. Stop making others responsible for your happiness.

Rise up and claim your rightful heritage, your true source, your unlimited inner power and abilities. Flush out the impurities by being fearless and undaunted by the ego's claim of triumph.

This is a restoration process—the restoration of you to your soul, your highest self.

If you have hidden agendas, designed by the ego, your progress will be limited. Waking up requires a strong focus and intent to reach your essence.

Do these things and you will be restored to your authentic self.

This is your spiritual assignment. It is an awesome journey. This book is intended to help you wake up. The impact it has on you is in your hands.

What is the measurement of your progress?

It is very simple. The results on your stage and life will be self-evident.

THE UNRAVELING OF THE DRAMA

As you become restored to your authentic self, you will no longer react to the drama in the workplace.

The other egos in the workplace may tend to escalate their own ego's behavior to try to gain a reaction from you. It is your reaction that is needed to keep reinforcing their ego identities.

The pressure to react, especially if the situation becomes hostile, is great because your ego is challenged. It will want to defend itself or even take the offense and attack what it believes is the source of the pain it is experiencing.

But it is only the ego that can feel this pain. Holding that calm space that is not from your ego is necessary in maintaining the peace during the other egos' attempt of increasing the drama on the workplace stage. This requires a lot of practice and patience with yourself because the temptation of the ego to be hooked is extremely strong.

Practice bringing yourself to the place of inner serenity every day. Resist reacting to others' egos. As you do, you will be heavily reinforced by a new inner confidence that comes from deep within your core. You will see a difference in yourself, the stage, and the other actors.

The ego's world is dependent on the reactions and re-reactions of others. When anyone then moves to begin to stop this insane interaction, the long-running play begins to break down. One by one, it begins to fall apart.

The engine that has been running out of control begins to run out of the fuel that is driving it down the track. The speeding train will ultimately come to a stop. It will take a while, depending on the speed and force with which it is traveling and the number of cars that are attached to it. But it will come to a stop . . . as leaders, one by one, initiate the process.

Without reactions from the ego identities, there is no drama. Without the drama being created, the performance is over.

The tragedy will end.

It will play out its last performance, and the players can then take their final bow.

The curtain will close.

At long last, the actors can take off their costumes and masks. The lights will go on, and the players will finally be restored to their inner greatness intended by the Creator.

Bravo! Bravo!

APPENDIX

PROFILE OF YOUR WORKPLACE

How Do You See Your Workplace?

This is a general survey designed to read the pulse of your company's heartbeat. For validity of this information, your answers must be very honest.

Its purpose is directed toward the tone and overall interaction that you find in your workplace environment. It is not intended to single out one specific individual.

Answers are totally confidential, but the results will be openly available.

Change cannot occur without knowledge, awareness, and acknowledgment. Let us thank you now for your interest and knowledge, candor and time to help promote a better workplace for all of us.

Please mark the boxes that indicate the attitudes or occurrences that you see or feel in your workplace:

ENERGY DEPLETING ENVIRONMENT

- ☐ Paranoia
- ☐ Insecurity
- ☐ Competition
- ☐ Blame
- ☐ Secrecy
- ☐ Discrimination
- ☐ Intimidation

- ☐ Sabotaging
- ☐ Power Struggles
- ☐ Fear
- ☐ Gossip
- ☐ Workaholism
- ☐ Personal Agendas
- ☐ Dishonesty

ENERGY CREATING ENVIRONMENT

- ☐ Open Communication
- ☐ Compassion
- ☐ Equality
- ☐ Appreciation
- ☐ Teamwork
- ☐ Job Security
- ☐ Integrity

- ☐ Fulfillment
- ☐ Trust
- ☐ Respect
- ☐ Responsive Management
- ☐ Clear Mission Statement
- ☐ Emotional Safety
- ☐ Fair Compensation

Tally Sheet for the Workplace Survey

From the survey "How Do You See Your Workplace," tally the number of responses for each attitude. In column B, tally each box that was checked. Then place the total in column C. In column D, write the total number of people who responded to the survey.

By dividing these totals, you will have a percentage for each attitude of how your people perceive their workplace.

The results will be in black and white. Now what? Is it time for enlightened leadership?

ENERGY DEPLETING ENVIRONMENT

A ATTITUDE	B RESPONSES ‖‖‖	C TOTAL	D TOTAL PEOPLE SURVEYED	E C ÷ D = %
Paranoia				
Insecurity				
Competition				
Blame				
Secrecy				
Discrimination				
Intimidation				
Sabotaging				
Power Struggles				
Fear				
Gossip				
Workaholism				
Personal Agendas				
Dishonesty				

Tally Sheet for the Workplace Survey

From the survey "How Do You See Your Workplace," tally the number of responses for each attitude. In column B, tally each box that was checked. Then place the total in column C. In column D, write the total number of people who responded to the survey.

By dividing these totals, you will have a percentage for each attitude of how your people perceive their workplace.

The results will be in black and white. Now what? Is it time for enlightened leadership?

ENERGY CREATING ENVIRONMENT

A ATTITUDE	B RESPONSES ⊞	C TOTAL	D TOTAL PEOPLE SURVEYED	E C ÷ D = %
Open Communication				
Compassion				
Equality				
Appreciation				
Teamwork				
Job Security				
Integrity				
Fulfillment				
Trust				
Respect				
Responsive Management				
Clear Mission Statement				
Emotional Safety				
Fair Compensation				

ABOUT THE AUTHOR

Danna Beal has been a manager, consultant, and trainer for nearly twenty years, based in Spokane, Washington. She received a Bachelor of Arts degree from Washington State University and graduated from Whitworth College with a Master's degree in Education.

Her interest in expanding human potential has been a thread throughout her life. She is committed to helping people everywhere rediscover their higher selves through a model that illuminates and brings clarity to the drama in the workplace.

Currently, she is teaching this new model for leadership in bringing spirit and compassion to the workplace. These seminars and workshops on enlightened leadership are available to businesses and organizations.

She is the founder of the Destiny Foundation, a non-profit organization whose mission is to create an institute, The Destiny Center for Leadership, dedicated to rebuilding relationships in the workplace.

The Destiny Foundation's goal is to create a center where companies and organizations can send their leaders for this training in a pristine environment that fosters understanding and receptivity.

Danna invites you to join her in this endeavor. To learn more, visit her internet sites at:

www.dbconsulting.com
www.spiritcenter.org